Scott's New

Handbook for Philatelists

Simon and Schuster
New York

Contents

1. Glossary of Philatelic Terms   7
2. Specialized Study Groups and Other
   Philatelic Societies   30
3. Foreign Currency Exchange   48
4. Magazines Around the World   55
5. The Road to Ribbons and Medals or How to
   Prepare Your Stamps for Exhibition   61
6. First Issues of the World   69
7. Using That Handiest Tool—the Catalogue   92
8. Stamp Identifier   99
9. Philatelic Literature—A Selective List   116
10. Postage Stamp Design: Prominent
    Americans Stamps of 1966   144
11. Index of U.S. Stamp Designers   160
12. Questions and Answers   165
13. Philatelic Agencies of the World   175
14. Country Names Change   185
    Index   186

CHAPTER 1

Glossary

of Philatelic Terms

STAMP COLLECTORS use many words and terms which have a peculiar meaning for their hobby. The following list, though incomplete, should help the average collector who wants to polish up his philatelic vocabulary and erase a few vague spots in his understanding of some of the finer points of the stamp game.

Acknowledgment of Receipt Stamp—A special stamp used to show the fee paid for the acknowledgment of receipt of a letter or other postal matter.

Adhesive—Stamp intended to be affixed to postal matter, as distinguished from one embossed or printed directly on an envelope, postal card or letter sheet.

Airmail or Airpost Stamps—Stamps specifically issued for use on airmail matter.

Airmail

Albino—A colorless, uninked impression of a stamp, usually an embossed envelope stamp, or of an overprint or surcharge on an adhesive stamp.

Aniline Color—A bright intense color, usually scarlet, rose or violet, derived from coal tar, which is water-soluble. *See* Fugitive Color.

Arrows—Arrow-shaped markings on sheet margins at end of guide lines, serving to guide printer, pane separator or perforator.

Authorized Delivery Stamps—Government stamps required to pay the additional fee for private delivery of a letter rather than through the post office. Used by Italy.

Backstamp—The marking applied to the back of an envelope to show the date and place of arrival at a receiving office.

Barred—Foreign stamps canceled with printed bars or parallel lines to show that they are no longer valid. A government practice with remainders sold to dealers below face.

Bâtonné Paper—Paper watermarked with straight, parallel lines a certain distance apart intended as a guide for writing. When the spaces between the lines are plain, the paper is called "wove bâtonné"; when the spaces are filled with less distinct parallel lines, it is termed "laid bâtonné."

Bicolored—Stamps printed in two colors.

Bilingual—Stamps having the inscription and value printed in two languages. Used in countries with two official languages, such as Canada, Belgium and South Africa.

Bilingual

Bisect—A stamp cut in half so that each part may be used separately to prepay postage. Used in emergencies when stamps of lower denomination were unavailable.

Bisect

Blocks—Unsevered units of four or more stamps, arranged at least two across and two deep.

Bogus—A label of private origin intended to deceive collectors; or a genuine stamp with unauthorized surcharge or overprint.

Bogus

Booklet Pane—A small pane, usually four, six or ten stamps, and usually printed in special sheets to be cut apart and fastened into booklets.

Bureau Prints—U.S. stamps precanceled at the Bureau of Engraving and Printing before being sent to local post offices for distribution.

Burelage—A network of dots or fine lines covering the face or back of a stamp to discourage counterfeiters.

Cachet—An impression generally applied to the face of an envelope to commemorate an event.

Canceled to Order ("C. T. O.")—Stamps canceled in quantities by governments with a view to selling them to collectors without giving any postal service in return.

Cancellation—A marking applied to a stamp to render it unfit for further use.

Cardboard—A form of Bristol board on which proof impressions are printed.

Carriers' Stamps—Stamps denoting this letter carriers' charge for the delivery of letters to and from a post office. In the early days the government postage franked a letter from one post office to another, but did not provide for delivery of letters from post office to addressee.

Carriers' Stamp

Centering—The placement of a stamp design with reference to the piece of paper on which it is printed. If the design is squarely in the center with four equal margins, it is said to be well centered.

Center Lines—Horizontal and vertical lines running through the center of a sheet of stamps for use as a guide in cutting and perforating.

Chalky Paper—Paper coated with a layer of glutinous

material and a white dust which, when dry and polished, has a glazed surface.

Charity Stamps—Receipts for funds collected for charity purposes. *See* Semipostal Stamps.

Classic

Classic—An issue which by virtue of its design, production, circumstances of use or rarity enjoys a position of distinction and singularity among stamps.

Clean-cut Perforation—A perforation in which the holes are cut out cleanly.

Cleaned—Describing a stamp from which the cancellation has been removed, either for reuse or for sale as an unused stamp.

Cliché—A single stereotype of a stamp design.

Coated Paper—*See* Chalky Paper.

Coils—Stamps issued in rolls for use in vending and affixing machines. They are perforated on two parellel sides in some countries and perforated on all sides in others.

Color Changeling—A stamp whose color has been altered, accidentally or intentionally, from the issued color, generally by chemicals or sunlight.

Color Trials—Printings in various colors made to facilitate selection of color for the issued stamp.

Comb Perforation—A perforation produced by a machine which has the pins so arranged as to perforate three sides of each stamp in a row at the same time.

Commemorative Issue—A special issue to celebrate some event or honor some person. Usually in circulation for a limited period.

Compound Perforations—Perforations which gauge differently on top and bottom than on the sides of a stamp (in "Perf. 11½ × 12," the 11½ is the horizontal measurement). In some instances

Commemorative

the perforation on one side may differ from that of the other three.

Condition—The quality of a stamp, determined by centering, cancellation, completeness, cleanliness, freshness of color, etc.

Control Mark—A letter or numeral placed either in the sheet margin or on the stamps by postal authorities as a check on the number of stamps in supply.

Counterfeit—An imitation of a stamp, prepared and distributed with intent to defraud.

Cover—The entire envelope or wrapping that has carried a letter through the mail.

Crease—A fold running through a stamp.

Cut Cancellation—A cancellation cutting through the stamp.

Cut Square—A stamp cut out with a square margin from a stamped envelope, postal card, wrapper or letter sheet.

Cut Square

Cut to Shape—A stamp trimmed to the very edge of its design.

Definitive

Definitive—A regular issue as distinguished from commemorative, semipostal, airmail or other issues.

Demonetized—Made invalid for postage by government decree.

Design—The printed part of the stamp as distinguished from the surrounding margin. Stamps may be of the same design but have differing inscriptions, country names or denominations.

Die—The original engraved piece of metal or other material from which reproductions are taken to form the plate for printing stamps.

Double Impression—A stamp showing a second impression distinctly overlapping the first.

Double Paper—An experimental paper made by pasting two sheets together. Also the overlapped paper produced when the paper roll used on a rotary press is spliced to a fresh roll.

Dry Printing—A refinement of U.S. stamp printing, begun in the 1950s, using thicker, stiffer paper than previously, special inks and greater pressure to force the paper into the recessed plates. Dry-printed stamps have whiter paper with high surface sheen, and the designs stand out sharply.

Duplex Cancellation—A cancellation in two parts: the date stamp and the canceling device.

Duty Plate—One of two plates used in producing bi-colored stamps. The duty plate prints the name and value, or value only. The head plate, or key plate, prints the rest of the design.

Early Impression—A stamp produced while the plate is new.

Electrotype—A method of producing replicas of a die by means of the electro deposit of copper upon a mold taken from such a die.

Embossed Stamps—Stamps in colored or uncolored relief; either the whole stamp or a part may be embossed.

Encased Postage Stamps—Stamps enclosed in special casings to be used as currency during coin shortages

Engraved Stamps—Stamps printed from metal plates into which a design is cut or etched.

Engraver's Proof—A trial printing made from an engraving to see how the stamp will look when finished.

Entire—A whole stamped envelope, letter sheet or wrapper, used or unused.

Error—A stamp with a mistake in the design, color, perforation or printing, unwittingly issued by the post office.

Essay—"A design essayed for a government stamp and differing in design in any particular from an officially issued stamp," wrote Clarence W. Brazer. "There are die essays, plate essays and experimental forms of essays."

Exhibition Pane—*See* Souvenir Sheets.

Expertize—To make an expert examination of a stamp.

Express Delivery Stamps—Special stamps to denote an extra charge for delivery by a special messenger. *See also* Special Delivery Stamp.

Face Value—The denomination or value shown on a stamp.

Facsimile—An imitation of a stamp represented as such.

Fakes—Stamps altered to resemble more valuable varieties by adding or cutting away perfora-

tions, cleaning, adding cancellations, etc. *See also* Counterfeit.

Fantasy—A bogus stamp.

Fine Perforation—A perforation having small holes and teeth close together.

First Day Cover—An envelope with stamp affixed canceled on day of issue. If dated since 1920, the cover should be canceled at the post office designated officially for the first day sale.

First Flight Cover—A cover with cancellation that shows the date and starting point of the first flight of a new airmail route.

Fiscal—A revenue stamp or a postage stamp with revenue cancellation.

Flat Plate—Stamps printed on the flat-bed press as distinguished from those printed with curved plates on the rotary press.

Forgery—*See* Counterfeit *and* Fakes.

Frame—The stamp's border, as distinct from the central design.

Franchise Stamps—Those issued and given by a government to certain private organizations to permit them to send their mail free.

Frank—A mark or label indicating postage paid, or the right of free postage.

Freak—A stamp differing from others of its kind due to paper creases, misplaced perforations, etc. An inconstant variety. Not an error.

Fugitive Color—A color that may run or fade when wet.

Goldbeater's Skin—A tough, transparent paper.

Granite Paper—Paper containing tiny, visible fibers.

Grid Cancellation—A cancellation usually made up of crisscrossed or diagonal lines usually within an oval.

Grill—A pattern of small dots impressed in the paper to break the surface and make it absorb canceling ink to prevent cleaning.

Grilled Gum—With the gumming, a light grilling process is sometimes applied to counteract the tendency to curl. It resembles a faint grill of vertical and horizontal ribs covering the entire back of the stamp, and can be seen after the gum has been removed.

Gripper Cracks—Cracks in rotary plates over the slots which receive the grippers to hold the underside of the plate to the press.

Guide Dots—Dots made on the plate or transfer roll as a guide in the correct spacing and alignment of stamps.

Guide Lines—*See* Center Lines.

Gum—The adhesive applied to the back of postage stamps.

Gum Breaker Bars—Colorless marks placed across the backs of some rotary press stamps during manufacture to prevent curling.

Gutters—Spaces between the panes of a sheet of stamps.

Handstamped—Stamped or canceled by hand.

Harrow Perforation—A perforation produced by a harrow machine, which does the whole sheet or pane in one operation.

Hatching—Close, fine lines that give shading to the design of a stamp.

Head Plate—*See* Duty Plate.

Hinge—A small piece of gummed paper used to mount stamps.

Hyphen Hole—A type of roulette perforation consisting of small rectangular holes resembling hyphens.

Imperforate

Imperforate (Imperf.)—A stamp without perforation or rouletting.

Impression—The actual printed design of a stamp.

Imprint—An inscription on a stamp below its design, or in the sheet margin. Usually it gives the printer's name or initials.

India Paper—A soft thin wove paper used for proof impressions.

Inscription—The name of the country, value, etc., inscribed on a stamp as distinct from its design.

Insurance Stamps—Stamps issued for use by a government's life insurance department.

Intaglio—Engraved.

Invert—A bicolored stamp with the center or frame printed upside down. The term also applies to an inverted overprint or surcharge.

Insurance

Joint Line Pair—On rotary coils, a line of color, not a guide line, showing between the stamps where the curved rotary plates meet or join on the press.

Invert

Killer—A heavy cancellation that covers most of the stamp.

Knife—The cutter of the machine which cuts out the envelope blank; also the size and shape of the die-cut papers from which envelopes are folded.

Laid Paper—A paper showing alternate light and dark parallel lines, crossed at right angles by more widely spaced lines caused by the arrangement of the wires in the dandy roll.

Late Fee Stamp—A stamp indicating payment of a special fee for forwarding a letter after the regular mail has been closed.

Letter Sheet—A sheet of paper bearing a printed stamp which can be folded to enclose the written message with the stamp and address on the outside.

Line Pair—A pair of stamps showing the guide line or joint line between them.

Lithography—A flat-surface printing method in which the design is drawn, photographed or transferred to a stone or metal plate in a greasy ink and fixed by treatment with acid. In printing, the stone is kept damp and the greasy ink image transfers to the paper.

Locals—Stamps issued for use in restricted areas either by governments or private posts.

Local

Local

Lozenge Roulette—A roulette in which the cuts are made in the shape of little crosses, diamonds or lozenges, with the outer corners open. Also called Diamond Roulette and *Percé en Losanges*.

Luminescent Stamps—Stamps coated or "tagged" with a colorless phosphorescent substance, or printed on fluorescent paper, or printed with fluorescent ink. Used with electronic machines to speed up mail processing.

Manila Paper—Strong, light paper, usually light brown, used for stamped envelopes and wrappers.

Manuscript Cancellation—A pen cancellation.

Margin—The paper surrounding the design of a stamp, souvenir sheet, small pane or large sheet.

Marginal Inscriptions—Inscriptions printed on the margin of a sheet.

Marginal Watermarks—Watermarks found in the margin of the stamp sheet. They may be the same as those on the stamps, or they may be the papermaker's name, etc.

Master Plate—A complete printing surface kept as a "master" from which to reproduce further plates.

Match and Medicine Stamps—Private-die proprietary stamps used in the U.S. in 1864–83 to pay the federal tax on patent medicines, matches, perfumes, playing cards and canned fruit.

Meter Stamp—A design printed directly on an envelope or card by a postage meter, indicating postage has been paid. This marking substitutes for an adhesive postage stamp.

Military

Military Stamps—Stamps issued for use by a country's miltary personnel.

Miniature Sheet—A small sheet consisting of one or a few stamps which have also been issued in a large·sheet. Usually the margin carries no in-

scription. A miniature sheet is not necessarily commemorative.

Mint—The condition of a stamp as released by the post office with fresh unfaded color, full perforations and original gum.

Mirror Print—The complete stamp design or part of it reversed as in a mirror. (Example: the Confederate States Postmaster's Provisional of Mt. Lebanon, La.)

Misstrike—A term used to denote envelope stamps impressed in the wrong place, partly impressed, or doubly printed.

Mixtures—Assortments of stamps unsorted, generally sold by weight and containing duplicates.

Moiré—A pattern of wavy lines resembling water silk printed on the face or back of a stamp to prevent removal of cancellation.

Mount—An accessory with acetate covering for mounting stamps and covers in an album without hinging them. May also be applied to a regular hinge.

Multiple Watermark—A watermark repeated so frequently in a sheet that parts of it appear several times on a single stamp.

Mute Cancellation—One which has no figures, lettering or inscription.

Native Paper—Paper of a tough fibrous nature, either wove or laid, used on early stamps of some Asiatic countries.

Newspaper Stamps—Stamps used for prepayment of postal charges on newspapers mailed in bulk.

Newspaper Tax Stamps—Stamps used on newspapers, originally denoting a tax, which later included postage.

Newspaper Stamp

Numeral Cancellation—An early type of cancellation which included a numeral instead of the place name at which the letter was posted.

Oblique Roulette—A roulette in which the cuts are set slanting, parallel to one another. Also called *Percé en Lignes Obliques.*

Obliteration—Cancellation.

Obsolete—Stamps which are no longer on sale at the post offices.

Occupation Stamps—Stamps forced upon a country during enemy occupation.

Official

Official Seals—Labels issued by a government to seal mail that has broken open in transit or been opened for postal inspection. These have no postal validity.

Official Stamps—Stamps issued for the free use of government officials.

Offset—An impression from the face of a wet sheet of stamps on the back of another sheet. The designs always appear reversed.

Offset Printing—A form of printing in which the designs are transferred to metal plates, the parts being raised that are to be inked.

On Cover—A stamp still on the envelope or wrapper as it was used in the mail.

Original Gum—The unimpaired gum on a stamp in the condition in which it left the post office.

Overprint—An inscription or device printed on a completed stamp. *See* Surcharge.

Oxidation—An unintended chemical process by which the original color of a stamp changes, as from orange to brown.

Overprint

Packet—A selection of stamps in a sealed envelope.

Packet Cancellation—A special cancellation or marking applied to mail carried aboard ship.

Pair—Two unseparated stamps.

Pane—A block of stamps surrounded by a margin and forming part of a sheet.

Parcel Post Stamps—Adhesives issued for use on parcel post matter.

Part Perforate—A stamp with incomplete perforation.

Parcel Post

Paste-up—The point where strips of stamps have been pasted together to make coils.

Patriotic Covers—Envelopes with special designs on the face, used during the Civil and Spanish-American Wars.

Pelure—A very thin hard tough paper, either wove or laid.

Penalty Envelopes—Envelopes used by U.S. Government departments for official mail. They require no postage and bear a warning of penalty for private use.

Perfins (Perforated Initials)—Stamps which have had small holes punched in them to form initials or devices, such as a crown. Private firms, universities and government departments or states have done this to prevent theft or to advertise. Perfins also include certain official stamps of Canada ("OHMS"), Australia ("OS"), Costa Rica (star), etc.

Perforated—With holes punched in the stamp margins to facilitate separation.

Perforation Gauge—A scale for determining the number of perforation holes in a 2-centimeter space.

Philatelic Agency—A bureau that sells stamps to col-

lectors, maintained by a government or a government-authorized private firm.

Philatelist—A collector who studies stamps, as distinguished from one who merely accumulates or speculates.

Philately—The study and collection of stamps as an avocation.

Phosphor Tagged—*See* Luminescent Stamps.

Photogravure—A process of printing in relief, the negative for which has been made by photographing the copy through a screen.

Pin Perforation—A roulette in which the paper is pierced by pinpoints without any paper being removed. Also called *Percé en Points*.

Plate—The base from which stamps are printed.

Plate Numbers—Serial numbers of plates found in margins of panes or sheets. On some 19th-century stamps of Britain, the plate number was incorporated in the stamp design.

Plate Proof—A trial impression made from a plate before the stamp printing begins.

Plate Variety—A variation from normal on the plate, usually caused by accident or retouching.

Plating—Arranging many copies of a stamp into the positions they originally occupied in the sheet or pane. This form of collecting is possible only on early issues where each stamp of a sheet had a certain characteristic variation.

Pneumatic Post—Mail carried between stations in cylinders propelled through tubes by compressed air.

Position Blocks—Blocks of four or more stamps, showing a certain position on the original sheet, such as arrow blocks, center line blocks, plate number blocks, etc.

Postage Currency—*See* Encased Postage Stamps.

Postage Due Stamps—Stamps placed on mail at the post office to show that the prepaid postage was inadequate.

Postal Fiscal—A stamp originally issued for revenue purposes, but allowed to be used as prepayment for postage.

Postage Due

Postally Used—Used for payment of postage, as distinguished from mint stamps, revenue stamps, or stamps canceled to order.

Postmark—A marking applied to a piece of mail in transit to designate its mailing point, date, or arrival.

Postmasters' Provisionals—Stamps issued by postmasters of various towns and cities before general issues were introduced by the government.

Precancels—Stamps canceled before use by being overprinted with the name of the place where they are to be used, with bars or other device. Used under permit by large mailers.

Printed on Both Sides—Describing a stamp with Printed impression both front and back as a result of feeding a sheet through the press twice. Not an offset (*q.v.*)

Precancel

Printers' Waste—Stamps spoiled in printing and not intended for use, but sometimes reaching collectors.

Private Die Proprietary Stamps—Stamps issued with government sanction by manufacturers to pay taxes on matches, medicine, playing cards, etc. *See* Match and Medicine Stamps.

Proof—A trial impression, taken to make certain that the printing plate, type, color, etc., are satisfactory before the main printing begins.

Provisionals—Stamps for use during shortages of regular issues. Usually prepared locally.

Quadrille Paper—Paper with a watermarked or printed pattern of crossed lines forming small squares or rectangles. (Example: France No. 103.)

Railroad Postmark—A cancellation or postal marking made on a railroad mail car, usually while the mail is in transit.

Reconstruction—*See* Plating.

Recutting—Strengthening or altering of lines on a plate by use of an engraving tool.

Redrawn—Said of an altered stamp design whose alteration requires the making of a new die.

Re-engraved—A term, like recut, describing alterations or additions to a die or plate which are more extensive than retouches.

Re-entry—A repair to a damaged, faint, worn or misaligned unit on a flat engraved plate. This is done by reapplying the transfer roller to the plate sometime after it has been finished. If any of the original details are not fully erased in the course of making the re-entry, they will show up as a double transfer on the stamp.

Registration Stamps—Stamps showing prepayment of a registration fee.

Regummed—Describing a stamp to which gum has been privately added to simulate the missing original gum.

Reissue—An official printing of a stamp after it has been withdrawn.

Remainders—Government-held stocks of stamps on hand after an issue has been withdrawn.

Repaired—Mended to improve the stamp's appearance or add to its value.

Reperforated—Privately "improved" by adding perforations to a straight edge, or by changing a common perforation gauge to a scarce one.

Reprints—Stamps printed from the original plates, usually after the issue has become obsolete, but not intended to be used for postage.

Retouch—A slight alteration of a die, cliché or plate which may have been worn or damaged.

Revalued—*See* Surcharge.

Revenue Stamps—Stamps issued for use in collecting special taxes. Fiscals.

Ribbed Paper—A wove paper having one side flat, the other side furrowed.

Revenue Stamp

Ripple Gum—*See* Grilled Gum.

Rotary Press Printing—A printing of stamps from curved plates on a rotary-type press. The stamps are slightly wider or taller than similar stamps printed from flat plates.

Rough Perforation—A ragged perforation.

Roulette—A means of stamp separation in which cuts are made in the paper without any part of it being removed. (In French, *Percé*.)

Ruled Paper—Paper ruled with faint, colored lines.

Safety Paper—A special paper used to make cleaning of a used stamp difficult.

Sample—An overprint sometimes applied to stamps instead of "Specimen" (*q.v.*).

Sawtooth Roulette—A form of roulette in which the cuts form small triangles. Also called *Percé en Scie*.

Secret Marks—Small marks placed on the original dies for identification purposes.

Semipostal Stamps—Stamps issued for the dual purpose of paying postage and raising funds for some special purpose.

Semipostal

Serpentine Roulette—A roulette formed of wavy cuts with small breaks between the curves. Also called *Percé en Serpentin.*

Serrated Roulette—A roulette in which the cuts are curved and the edges show little scallops. Also called Arc Roulette, *Percé en Arc,* and Serrated Perforation.

Serrated Roulette

Set—A number of stamps belonging to a particular issue or series.

Se-tenant—Stamps of different designs or values, or stamps with and without overprints, which are joined and printed as a pair.

Se-tenant

Shade—A slight variation of the normal color.

Sheet—A complete sheet of stamps, as printed, before being cut apart into panes.

Sheet Watermark—A watermark so large that only a small part of it may be found on a single stamp.

Silk Paper—Paper containing colored silk fibers.

Silk Thread Paper—Paper with continuous silk threads running through the sheet in parallel lines, one or more appearing on each stamp.

Silurian Paper—*See* Granite Paper.

Skinned—To describe a stamp which has lost some of its paper, leaving a thin spot.

Souvenir Sheets—Sheets of a small number of stamps in the same or different design, generally with marginal inscriptions relating to the event the stamps commemorate.

Souvenir Sheet

Special Delivery Stamp—A stamp issued to insure delivery of mail in advance of regular delivery.

Specialist—A collector who specializes in a particular class or kind of stamps.

Special Delivery

Special Printing—Stamps of current designs or reissues printed for some special purpose.

Specimen—An overprint or punching found on stamps intended for distribution as a sample of a new issue.

Speculative Issues—Stamps unnecessary for postal requirements, made principally for sale to collectors.

Split Grill—A stamp showing parts of two grills.

Specimen

Stampless Covers—Postmarked envelopes or folded letters that passed through the mails before stamps came into use.

Surcharge

Straight Edge—The imperforate side of a stamp which has not been perforated on four sides.

Strip—Three or more unsevered stamps in a vertical or horizontal row.

Surcharge—An overprint which changes or restates the value of a stamp.

Surtax—A charge in addition to the postage, such as that indicated on semipostal stamps.

Syncopated Perforation—One which is not regular, but has gaps in the lines of perforations. Also called Interrupted Perforation. Used by Netherlands.

Teeth—The projections between perforation holes.

Telegraph Stamps—Stamps used to prepay telegraph tolls.

Tête-bêche—A pair of unseparated stamps, one of which is printed upside down in relation to the other.

Tête-Bêche

Tied—Refers to adhesive stamps on cover or piece where part of the cancellation extends beyond the stamp, tying it to the cover or piece.

Tongs—Metal tweezers for handling stamps easily, quickly and without damage.

Too Late Stamp—*See* Late Fee Stamp.

Typographed—Printed from type or from plates on which the lines of the design are raised.

Unused—Not canceled or otherwise defaced. The unused stamp need not have gum or be in mint condition.

Unwatermarked—Showing no watermark.

Used—Canceled or postmarked. Usually a stamp which has done postal duty. This term is also applied (incorrectly) to a stamp that has been favor-canceled or canceled to order.

Variety—A stamp showing differences from the normal.

Varnish Bars—Lines or bars of colorless varnish applied to the face of a stamp to discourage cancellation removal.

Vignette—The central portrait, picture, or other main feature of a stamp's design as distinguished from its frame.

Watermark

War Tax Stamps—Stamps issued in wartime to collect a tax on letters.

Watermark—A design, mark or lettering worked into the paper during manufacture.

Wet Printing—The use in printing of paper which has a certain moisture content.

Zigzag Roulette—Roulette in which cuts are made to produce sharp points along the edge of the stamps. Also called *Percé en Pointes*.

CHAPTER 2

Specialized Study Groups and Other Philatelic Societies

THE LONER obviously misses much of the philatelic fun and comradeship with fellow pilgrims in his chosen field. If he joins at least one general society and one specialist group—besides the local stamp club, of course—he will not only find such fellowship but he will learn much more about his favorite stamps. He will also have a chance to give—a chance to help others by sharing *his* knowledge and discoveries.

The good specialist society reacts kindly to the groper pursuing the elusive fact. It is willing to help by answering the queries of nonmembers as well as those of its own members. It realizes this is a sound way to grow.

The variety of stamp organizations is amazing. There is even one devoted exclusively to flag cancellations.

Most of the specializing study groups are well-run societies with a backbone of completely dedicated practitioners. They often strain themselves to keep this great hobby rolling smoothly.

AIRMAILS (*see also* individual countries)
Aeronautica and Air Label Collectors Club, LeRoy V. Coburn, Box 69, Bomoseen, Vt.

Aero Philatelists, Inc., William N. Mead, 8707 Crefeld St., Philadelphia, Pa. 19118. Publishes *The Aero Philatelist Annals.*

American Air Mail Society, Mrs. Ruth T. Smith, 102 Arbor Rd., Cinnaminson, N. J. 08077. Publishes *The Airpost Journal.*

Independent Space and Rocket Mail Club, Bill Ronson, 132 Nassau St., New York, N. Y. 10038.

Jack Knight Air Mail Society, Earl H. Wellman, 3532 Oak Ave., Brookfield, Ill. 60513. Official organ, *Jack Knight Air Log.*

Rocket Mail Society, Earl Wellman, 3532 Oak Ave., Brookfield, Ill. 60513.

ALASKA

Alaskan Collectors Club, Lowell V. Holmes, 3830 Twana Dr., Des Moines, Iowa 50310. Publishes *The Alaskan Philatelist.*

ALBANIA

Albanian Philatelic Society, S. Samuel Nukes, 803 Akron Savings and Loan Bldg., Akron, Ohio 44308.

AUSTRALIA

Australian Commonwealth Collectors' Club of New South Wales, C. Ashworth-Spreat, 3 Godfrey St., Artarmon, N.S.W., Australia. Publishes *The Bulletin.*

Australian Commonwealth Specialists' Society of Great Britain, V. W. Dix, 8 Shandon Close, Tunbridge Wells, Kent, England. Publishes *News and Notes* and *The Bulletin.*

Society of Australasian Specialists, Robert L. Cocklin, 1638 19th St., Cuyahoga Falls, Ohio 44223. Publishes *The Australasian Informer.*

AUSTRIA

Austria Philatelic Society of New York, Leopold Kovacs, 75-55 Utopia Parkway, Jamaica, N. Y.

Austrian Stamp Club, James W. Syddall, 21 Moscow Rd., Edgeley, Stockport, Cheshire, England.

AUTOGRAPHS

Universal Autograph Collector's Club, Richard Grayson, 7 Walden Ave., Jericho, N. Y. 11753. Publishes *The Pen and Quill.*

BELGIAN CONGO

Belgian Congo Study Circle, R. H. Keach, 25 Kingswood Rd., Tadworth, Surrey, England. Publishes *The Bulletin.*

BELGIUM

Belgium Study Circle, T. A. Jones, 25 Park Rd., Ramsgate, Kent, England. Publishes *Newsletter.*

BOOKLETS

Airmail Booklet Collectors Club, John Jezek, Jr., 3532 Oak Ave., Brookfield, Ill.

Booklet Pane Society, 6769 Groton St., Forest Hills, N. Y. 11375. Publishes *The Booklet.*

BRAZIL

Clube Filatelico do Brasil, Dr. Carlos Nery da Costa, Caixa Postal 195, Rio de Janeiro, Brazil. Publishes *Brasil Filatelico* and *Boletim do Brasil Filatelico.*

BRITISH COMMONWEALTH (*see also* individual countries)

British Commonwealth Philatelic Study Club, Daniel W. Vooys, P. O. Box 187, Canajoharie, N. Y. 13317. Publishes *The Bulletin.*

British Empire Study Group, Richard S. Wilson, 92 Dennis St., Manhasset, N. Y. 11030.

King George VI Collectors' Society, Frank R. Saunders, 65 Westbrook Ave., West Hartlepool, Co. Durham, England. Publishes *The Newsletter.*

BRITISH NORTH AMERICA (*see also* individual countries)

British North American Philatelic Society, Jack Levine, 7061 Old King's Road So., Jacksonville, Fla. 32217. Publishes *B.N.A. Topics.*

BRITISH WEST AFRICA

British West Africa Study Circle, H. B. MacMillan, Rowditch Printing Works, Derby, England.

CANADA

Canadian Airmail Collectors' Club, Earl Wellman, 3532 Oak Ave., Brookfield, Ill. 60513.

Canadian Philatelic Society of Great Britain, Dr. C. W. Hollingsworth, 17 Mellish Rd., Walsall, Staffs., England. Publishes *Maple Leaves.*

CANCELLATIONS AND POSTMARKS

American Naval Cancellation Society, Inc., Box 101, Wildwood, N. J. 08260. Publishes *Naval Covers.*

British Postmark Society, G. R. Pearson, 42 Corrance Rd., London S. W. 2, England. Publishes *The Bulletin.*

First Flight Federation, Horace D. Westbrooks, P. O. Box 252, Griffin, Ga. 30223.

Flag Cancel Society, Harry S. Taber, Sidney Center, N. Y. 13839. Publishes *Flag Cancellations.*

Fourth Class Cancellation Club, William F. Rapp, Jr., 430 Ivy Ave., Crete, Neb. 68333. Publishes *Newsletter.*

Maritime Postmark Society, Alan T. Tattersall, 2542 Treemont St., Jacksonville, Fla. Publishes *Seaposter.*

Mobile Post Office Society, Warren F. Kinball, Jr., 163 Old Farm Rd., Pleasantville, N. Y. 10507. Publishes *The Transit Postmark Collector.*

Postmark Collectors' Club, Robert K. Francis, 11 Jeralds Ave., Yalesville, Conn. 06492. Publishes *PMCC Bulletin.*

T. P. O. and Seapost Society, Cyril Kidd, 9 Beech Park Ave., Northenden, Manchester 22, England. Publishes *T.P.O. Magazine.*

Universal Ship Cancellation Society, Albert O. Wickard, 9168 Rockland Ave., Detroit, Mich. 48239. Publishes *U.S.C.S. Log.*

CEYLON

Ceylon Philatelic Society, M. T. H. Johar, 85 Chatham St., Colombo, Ceylon. Publishes *Ceylon Stamp Journal.*

CHARITY STAMPS AND SEALS

Christmas Seal & Charity Stamp Society, J. L. Cooprider, 170 S. E. 3rd St., Linton, Ind. 47441. Publishes *Seal News.*

CHILE

Sociedad Filatélica de Chile, Derek Palmer, Casilla 13245, Santiago, Chile. Publishes *Chile Filatélico.*

CHINA

China Philatelic Society of London, P. W. Locke, 74 Ellerton Rd., Wandsworth Common, London S. W. 18, England. Publishes *The Journal of Chinese Philately.*

China Stamp Society, Charles W. Dougan, 9082 Vons Dr., Garden Grove, Calif. 92641. Publishes *The China Clipper*.

COLOMBIA

Club Filatélico de Barranquilla, Fernando Avendaño M., Apartado Aereo 685, Barranquilla, Colombia. Publishes *Filba*.

COSTA RICA

Asociación Filatélica de Costa Rica, Francisco Chaves S., Apartado 3441, San José, Costa Rica. Publishes *Costa Rica Filatélica*.

Society of Costa Rica Collectors, Arthur L. Hebel, P. O. Box 407, Novato, Calif. 94947. Publishes *The Oxcart*.

COVERS

American First Day Cover Society, Marge Finger, P. O. Box 23, Elberon, N. J. 07740. Publishes *First Days*.

Universal Philatelic Cover Society, Kenneth D. Paulson, Box 2325, Overland, Mo. 63114. Publishes *Universal Cover News*.

War Cover Club, Thomas McGrath, 804 Park Ave., Albany, N. Y. 12208. Publishes *The Bulletin*.

Western Cover Society, B. C. Pierce, 305 Sheridan Ave., Piedmont, Calif. 94611. Publishes *Western Express*.

CZECHOSLOVAKIA

Czechoslovak Philatelic Society of North America, Frank J. Kosik, Route 1, Box 286, Delavan, Wis. 53115. Publishes *Czechoslovak Specialist*.

EGYPT

Egyptian Philatelic Society, Ernest A. Kehr, 220 W. 42nd St., New York, N. Y. 10036. Publishes *E.P.S. Newsletter*.

Egypt Study Circle, Ernest H. Proctor, 4 Eden Rd., Tunbridge Wells, Kent, England. Publishes a circular quarterly.

Philatelic Society of Egypt, P. O. Box 142, Cairo, Egypt. Publishes *L'Orient Philatélique*.

ESSAYS AND PROOFS

Essay-Proof Society, Inc., Kenneth Minuse, 1236 Grand Concourse, New York, N. Y. 10456. Publishes *The Essay-Proof Journal*.

FRANCE

France and Colonies Philatelic Society, Inc., Gilbert R. Loisel, 88-11 34th Ave., Jackson Heights, N. Y. 10072. Publishes *France and Colonies Philatelist.*

GERMANY

Germany Philatelic Society, Inc., Mrs. Johanna E. Schaefer, P. O. Box 88, Valparaiso, Ind. 46383. Publishes *The German Postal Specialist.*

Third Reich Study Group, Kenneth J. David, 95 Courtland St., Worcester, Mass. 01602. Publishes *The Bulletin.*

GREAT BRITAIN

Great Britain Philatelic Society, P. J. D'Arcy, 67 Cissbury Ring South, London N. 12, England.

Great Britain Study Circle, J. W. Brewer, "Downview," 1, the Ridgewaye, Southborough, Tunbridge Wells, Kent, England.

GREECE

Hellenic Philatelic Society of America, Dr. Maurice B. Friend, 262 Central Park West, New York, N. Y. 10024. Publishes *Bulletin.*

GUATEMALA

Asociación Filatélica de Guatemala, José Marcelino Zamora, Apartado Postal 1529, Guatemala City, Guatemala. Publishes *Guatemala Filatélica.*

International Society of Guatemala Collectors, Romeo J. Routhier, Edificio El Cielito, Apartado 307, Zona 1, Guatemala City, Guatemala. Publishes *El Quetzal.*

HONG KONG

Hong Kong Study Circle, W. R. Welleted, Langite Works, South Chingford, London E. 4, England. Publishes *The Bulletin.*

INDIA

India Study Circle, B. T. Cheverton, 42 Ashcroft Rd., Luton, England. Publishes *The Bulletin.*

Indo-American Philatelic Society of Hyderabad, Dr. S. M. Hyder Raza Zaidi, O. U. 7/12 Jamai Osmania, Hyderabad 7, A. P., India. Publishes *The Hyderabad Philatelist.*

Philatelic Society of India, D. E. Wadia, Shireen Mansion, Tardeo P. O. Bldg., Tardeo, Bombay, India. Publishes *The Philatelic Journal of India*.

IRAQ

Iraqi Philatelic Society, Saib Al-Jassany, Scheherazade Building, South Gate, Baghdad, Iraq. Publishes *Stamp World*.

IRELAND

Eire Philatelic Association, Gil P. Roberts, Jr., 1716 West Alpine Ave., Stockton, Calif. 95204. Publishes *The Revealer*.

ISRAEL

British Association of Palestine-Israel Philatelists, B. A. Remington, 36 Sinclair Grove, London N. W. 11, England. Publishes *The Bulletin*.

Israel-Palestine Philatelic Society of America, Miss Frances F. Goodman, 6161 N. Winthrop Ave., Chicago, Ill. 60626. Publishes *The Bulletin*.

Judaica Historical Philatelic Society, Sidney Bernstein, 18 W. 70th St., New York, N. Y. 10023. Publishes *Judaica Philatelic Journal*.

Society of Israel Philatelists, Arthur Engers, 40-67 61st St., Woodside, N. Y. 11377. Publishes *The Israel Philatelist*.

JAMAICA

Jamaica Study Group, Howard J. Gaston, College Highway, Granby, Conn. 06035. Publishes *The Bulletin*.

JAPAN

International Society for Japanese Philately, Inc., Mrs. William Evans, 107 Winthrop Rd., Brookline, Mass. 02146. Publishes *Japanese Philately*.

Japanese-American Philatelic Society, George Kinnear, 1691 Alvarado Ave., Apt. 31, Walnut Creek, Calif. 94596. Publishes *The Postal Bell*.

KOREA

Korea Stamp Society, Forrest W. Calkins, P. O. Box 1057, Grand Junction, Colo. 81501. Publishes *Korean Philately*.

LIECHTENSTEIN
Liechtenstein Study Circle, Jack Beken, 30 Lingwood Gardens, Isleworth, Middlesex, England. Publishes *The Bulletin.*

LITHUANIA
Lithuanian Philatelic Society, A. Ruzgas, 87-37 78th St., Woodhaven, N. Y. Publishes *The Bulletin.*

LUXEMBOURG
Luxembourg Philatelic Study Club, Warren W. Sadler, 219 Governor St., Richmond, Va. Publishes *The Luxembourg Philatelist.*

MALAYA
Malaya Study Group, Howard J. Selzer, 5035C. W. Jackson Blvd., Chicago, Ill. 60644. Publishes *The Malayan Philatelist.*

MALTA
Malta Study Circle, M. E. Jetten, 25 Hereford Court, Danesgate, Wealdstone, Harrow, Middlesex, England. Publishes *Malta Newsletter* and *Study Papers.*

MASONS
Masonic Stamp Club of New York, Inc., Samuel Brooks, 985 Anderson Ave., Bronx, N. Y. Publishes *Masonic Philatelist.*

METERS AND SLOGANS
American Metered Postage Society, Henry O. Meisel, Clintonville, Wis. 54929. Publishes *The Indicia News.*

Meter Stamp Society, William E. Pamperien, 1617 N. E. 5th St., Fort Lauderdale, Fla. 33304. Publishes *The Bulletin.*

Postal Slogan Cancel and Meter Society, Moe Luff, 12 Greene Rd., Spring Valley, N. Y. 10977. Publishes *Slogan Slants* and *Meters & Collectors.*

MEXICO
Elmhurst Philatelic Society, Peter Sognefest, 2336 S. 10th Ave., Broadview, Ill. Publishes *Mexicana.*

Mexican Airmail Collectors Club, Earl Wellman, 3532 Oak Avenue, Brookfield, Ill. 60513.

NETHERLANDS

Netherlands and Colonies Philatelists, Johannes de Kruyf, 45 Quincy Lane, Bergenfield, N. J. 07621. Publishes *Netherlands and Colonial Philately*.

NEW ZEALAND

New Zealand Society of Great Britain, G. E. C. Pratt, 32A The Ridgeway, Sutton, Surrey, England. Publishes *The Kiwi*.

NICARAGUA

Sociedad Filatélica de Nicaragua, Ernesto Kelly, Av. Bolívar 512, Managua, Nicaragua. Publishes *Revista Filatélica*.

ORANGE FREE STATE

Orange Free State Study Circle, W. B. Marriott, 46 Kingswood Gardens, Leeds 8, Yorkshire, England. Publishes *O.F.S. Bulletin*.

PACIFIC ISLANDS

Pacific Islands Study Circle of Great Britain, Albert E. Young, 58 Livesay Crescent, Worthing, Sussex, England. Publishes *Pacifica*.

PAKISTAN

Pakistan Philatelic Association, M. Sharif Qurshi, 42 The Mall, Lahore, Pakistan. Publishes *Pakistan Stamps*.

Pakistan Philatelic Study Group, Jeanne B. Pogue, 23 Grove St., New York, N. Y. 10014. Publishes *Pakphil Newsletter*.

Pakistan Study Circle, B. T. Cheverton, 42 Ashcroft Road, Luton, England.

PAN-AMERICA

Pan-American Collectors Club, William Bolle, 9121 91st Ave., Woodhaven, N. Y.

PAPUA AND NEW GUINEA

Papuan Philatelic Society, W. H. Colbran, 66 Sussex Rd., Haywards Heath, Sussex, England. Publishes *Stamp News*.

PERFINS

Perfins Club, F. C. Neal, 11209 Walnut St., El Monte, Calif. 91731. Publishes *Perfins Bulletin*.

Security Endorsement & Perfin Society of Great Britain, R. Bowman, "Gwel Marten," Beechfield Rd., Frilsham, Newbury, Berks., England.

PERSIA
Persian Study Circle, Bernard Lucas, 99 Moseley Wood Dr., Cookridge, Leeds 16, England.

PERU
Asociación Filatélica Peruana, Luis Guzmán P., Los Mogaburu 269, Lima, Peru. Publishes *Filatelia Peruana.*

PHILATELIC EXHIBITIONS
Association of Stamp Exhibitions, Charles S. Lasky, 162-05 89th Ave., Jamaica, N. Y. 11432. Publishes *The Daybook.*

PHILATELIC LITERATURE
Philatelic Literature Association, Daniel W. Vooys, P. O. Box 187, Canajoharie, N. Y. 13317. Publishes *Philatelic Literature Review.*

PHILIPPINES
Asociación Filatélica de Filipinas, Fabian Carmona, Jr., P. O. Box 2405, Manila, Philippines. Publishes *A. F. F. Journal.*

POLAND
Polonus Philatelic Society, Roman H. Strzelecki, 1439 N. Bell Ave., Chicago, Ill. 60622. Publishes *Polonus Bulletin.*

PORTUGAL
International Society for Portuguese Philately, Mrs. G. L. Perryman, 8941 Burlington Blvd., Brookfield, Ill. 60513. Publishes *Portu-Info.*

POSTAL HISTORY
Bahamas Postal History Study Circle, G. J. Raymond, P. O. Box 35143, Houston, Texas. Publishes *Bahamas News Notes.*

Postal History Society of the Americas, Mrs. Edith M. Faulstich, 37 Inwood St., Yonkers, N. Y. 10704. Publishes *Postal History Journal* and *Postal History Digest.*

Postal History Society of Great Britain, Frederick Walker, June Cottage, North St., Petworth, Sussex, England. Publishes *The Bulletin*.

Wisconsin Postal History Society, Charles J. Peirce, 1312 Ontario St., Oshkosh, Wis. Publishes *Badger Postal History*.

POSTAL STATIONERY

United Postal Stationery Society, Gordon C. Morison, 120 Klink Rd., Rochester, N. Y. 14625. Publishes *Postal Stationery*.

POSTCARDS

Metropolitan Postcard Collectors Club, Joseph J. Nardone, 436 E. 9th St., New York, N. Y. 10009. Publishes *The Bulletin*.

PRECANCELS

National Association of Precancel Collectors, Inc., Glenn W. Dye, 5200-08 Arctic Ave., Wildwood, N. J. 08260. Publishes *The Precancel Stamp Collector* and *Modern Type Chart of Precancellations*.

Precancel Stamp Society, Inc., O. E. Frost, P. O. Box 1743, Wheaton Station, Silver Springs, Md. Publishes *The Precancel Forum*.

REPLY COUPONS

Reply Coupon Collectors' Society, Dr. Allan Hauck, 1640 N. Monroe St., Fremont, Neb. 68025. Publishes *Reply Coupon Collector*.

REVENUES

American Revenue Association, Frank Q. Newton, 6730 N. Temple City Blvd., Arcadia, Calif. 91006. Publishes *The American Revenuer*.

RHODESIA

Rhodesian Study Circle, F. C. Donaldson, 14 Makepeace Ave., Highgate, London N. 6, England. Publishes *The Journal*.

RUSSIA

British Society of Russian Philately, John Lloyd, The Retreat, Queens' Road, West Bergholt, Colchester, Essex, England. Publishes *British Journal of Russian Philately*.

Rossica Society of Russian Philately, Rimma A. Sklarevski, 640 N. Charles St. Ave., Towson, Md. 21204. Publishes *The Journal*.

Russian American Philatelic Club, Herman Shenitz, 31-15 33rd St., Long Island City, N. Y. 11106. Publishes *The Russian Philatelist*.

RYUKYU ISLANDS

International Ryukyu Stamp and Coin Society, James N. Wong, P. O. Box 75666, Los Angeles, Calif. 90005. Publishes *IRSACS Bulletin*.

Ryukyu Collectors Club, Stewart Kusinitz, 10 Bartlett St., Malden, Mass. 02148. Publishes *RCC Bulletin*.

SARAWAK

Sarawak Specialists' Society, K. G. Basden, 48 Blackborough Rd., Reigate, Surrey, England. Publishes *The Stamps and Postal History of Sarawak*.

SCANDINAVIA

Scandinavian Collectors Club, 1625 W. 104th Place, Chicago, Ill. Publishes *The Post Horn*.

Scandinavian Philatelic Society, H. T. Pritchett, 3 Mark's Ave., Ongar, Essex, England. Publishes *The Scandinavian Contact*.

SHEETS

Miniature Reconstructed Sheet Society, Robert N. Pritchard, P. O. Box 691, Aurora, Ill. 60507. Publishes *Margin Edge*.

SOUTH AFRICA

Philatelic Federation of South Africa, S. J. Vermaak, P. O. Box 375, Johannesburg, South Africa. Publishes *The South African Philatelist*.

South African Collectors' Society, W. A. Page, 138 Chastilian Rd., Dartford, Kent, England. Publishes *Springbok*.

SPAIN

Spanish Civil War Study Group, Theodore Van Dam, 1122 E. 180th St., Bronx, N. Y. 10460. Publishes *Cruzada*.

Spanish Study Circle, Miss E. W. Faris, Poplars, Theydon Bois, Epping, Essex, England. Publishes *España*.

SWITZERLAND

Helvetia Philatelic Society, Edith M. Faulstich, 37 Inwood St., Yonkers, N. Y. 10704.

Helvetia Philatelic Society (of Great Britain), Mrs. E. J. Rawnsley, 32 Ethelbert Gardens, Gants Hill, Ilford, Essex, England. Publishes *Helvetia Newsletter*.

THAILAND

Thailand Philatelic Society, P. E. Collins, 85 St. John's Rd., Woking, Surrey, England. Publishes *Thai Times*.

TOPICALS

American Topical Association, Jerome Husak, 3306 N. 50th St., Milwaukee, Wis. 53216. Publishes *Topical Times*.

Americana Unit of A.T.A., Russell M. Mohney, 21 Orchard St., Wheatland, Pa. 16161.

Biology Unit of A.T.A., Dr. Willard F. Stanley, State University College, Fredonia, N. Y. 14063. Publishes *Bio-Philately*.

Dwight D. Eisenhower Postal Society, Frank Watt, P. O. Box 1176, Waco, Texas. Publishes *The Bulletin*.

Engineering Unit of A.T.A., William D. French, 67 Stratton St., Yonkers, N. Y. 10701.

Europa Study Unit of A.T.A., Donald W. Smith, 1633 Florida Ave., Johnstown, Pa. 15902. Publishes *Europa News*.

Fine Arts Unit of A.T.A., Dr. John S. Papa, 1950 N. E. 59th Place, Fort Lauderdale, Fla. 33308. Publishes *Fine Arts Philatelist*.

Geology Study Unit of A.T.A., Martin Koenig, 1245 E. 22nd St., Brooklyn, N. Y. 11210. Publishes *The Geo-Philatelist*.

Journalism Unit of A.T.A., Walter Everett, 11 River Glen, Hastings-on-Hudson, N. Y.

John F. Kennedy Philatelic Society, George H. Goldey, P. O. Box 337, Canton, Texas 75103. Publishes *New Frontier News*.

Lincoln Society of Philately, Julian Graff, 2112-A St. John's Ave., Highland Park, Ill. 60035. Publishes *The Lincoln Log*.

Lions Philatelic Unit of A.T.A., Russell H. Eliot, 91-A Main St., Foxboro, Mass. Publishes *The Philatelion*.

Map Stamp Unit of A.T.A., Miss Edythe F. Bull, R. F. D. 3, West Redding, Conn. 06896. Publishes *The Carto-Philatelist*.

Medical Subjects Unit of A.T.A., Mrs. Myrtle I. Watt, 5293 Jasmine Circle North, St. Petersburg, Fla. 33712. Publishes *Scalpel and Tongs.*

Casey Jones Railroad Unit of A.T.A., Margaret M. Park, 10-200 Avenida Serena N. W., Paradise Hills, Albuquerque, New Mexico 87114. Publishes *The Dispatcher.*

Collectors of Religion on Stamps (COROS), Gertrude Jiracek, 1222 Travis St., La Crosse, Wis. 54601. Publishes *COROS Chronicle.*

Marian Philatelic Study Group of COROS, W. J. Hoffman, 424 W. Crystal View Ave., Orange, Calif. 92667. Publishes *The Marian Philatelist.*

Franklin D. Roosevelt Philatelic Society, Gustav Detjen, Jr., P. O. Box 172, Hyde Park, N. Y. 12538. Publishes *Fireside Chats.*

Scout Stamps Collectors' Club, Howard L. Fears, 6 Claremont Road, Seaford, Sussex, England.

Scouts on Stamps Society International, Jay L. Rogers, 37 Spindle Rd., Hicksville, N. Y. 11801. Publishes *SOSSI Journal.*

Ships on Stamps Unit of A.T.A., Miss Emily M. Condit, 260 Watchung Ave., Orange, N. J. 07050. Publishes *Watercraft Philately.*

Space Unit of A.T.A., W. H. Winslow, P. O. Box 627, Tarpon Springs, Fla. 33589. Publishes *The Astrophile.*

Sports Philatelists International, L. K. Eichorn, 18502 Winslow Rd., Shaker Heights, Ohio 44122. Publishes *The Journal of Sports Philately.*

Stamps on Stamps—Centenary Unit of A.T.A., Harold Arnold, 1328 Brinkley Ave., Los Angeles, Calif. 90049. Publishes *Signal.*

TRANSVAAL

Transvaal Study Circle, Maj. H. M. Criddle, 23 Longcroft Ave., Banstead, Surrey, England. Publishes *The Transvaal Philatelist.*

TRINIDAD

Trinidad Philatelic Society, Harold E. Box, 2 First Ave., Cascade, Port of Spain, Trinidad, W. I. Publishes *The Bulletin.*

UNITED NATIONS

United Nations Philatelic Society, David S. J. Alexander, United Nations, N. Y. Publishes *The Bulletin.*

United Nations Study Unit of A.T.A., Martin Hoff, 59-16 Grove St., Brooklyn, N. Y. 11227. Publishes *United Nations Bulletin*.

UNITED STATES

AHPS-CWPS (American Historical Philatelic Society and Civil War Philatelic Society), Lincoln Center Offices, Box 2A, 41 Central Park West, New York, N. Y. 10023. Publishes *The Blue and the Grey*.

Bureau Issues Association, Inc., Esther H. Sullivan, 38 Gray St., Arlington, Mass. 02174. Publishes *The United States Specialist*.

Civil War Philatelic Society, Doris Raciti, King George Road, Warren Township, Plainfield, N. J. Publishes *The Blue and the Grey*.

Confederate Stamp Alliance, Billy Matz, Box 12162, Memphis, Tenn. 38112. Publishes *Confederate Philatelist*.

U. S. 1851–60 Unit, Melvin W. Schuh, 6 Laconia Road, Worcester, Mass. 01609.

U. S. Locals Collectors, Box 121, Wildwood, N. J. 08260. Publishes *Local Posts* and *The American Hobbyist*.

U. S. Philatelic Classics Society, Inc., Melvin W. Schuh, 6 Laconia Road, Worcester, Mass. 01609. Publishes *The Chronicle of U. S. Classic Postal Issues*.

UNLISTED MATERIAL

(Locals, Fantasies, Forgeries, Bogus, Labels, etc.)

Cinderella Stamp Club, Ira Zweifach, 336 Central Park West, New York, N. Y. 10025. Publishes *Cinderella Philatelist*.

S. Allen Taylor Society, Paul Gapp, 185 Westwood Dr., Park Forest, Ill. 60466. Publishes *The Journal*.

URUGUAY

Club Filatélico del Uruguay, Julio A. Castelnuovo, Casilla Correo 1707, Montevideo, Uruguay. Publishes *Uruguay Filatélico*.

Uruguay Collectors Club, Herman Kerst, 310 Woodbridge Road, Des Plaines, Ill.

VATICAN

Vatican Philatelic Society, Wallace R. Smith, 165-15 Union Turnpike, Flushing, N. Y. 11366. Publishes *Vatican Notes*.

VENEZUELA

Club Filatélico de Caracas, Dr. Pedro José D. Espejo, Apartado 8, Caracas, Venezuela. Publishes *Revista del Club Filatélico de Caracas.*

GENERAL SOCIETIES

American Philatelic Congress, Inc., Robert B. Brandeberry, 58 W. Salisbury Dr., Wilmington, Del. 19809. Publishes *American Philatelic Congress Annual Book.*

American Philatelic Society, Inc., James T. DeVoss, P. O. Box 800, State College, Pa. 16801. Publishes *The American Philatelist.*

ATOZ Stamp Club, John H. Thomas, 10 East 138th St., New York, N. Y. 10037.

British Philatelic Association, Ltd., 446 Strand, London W. C. 2, England. Publishes *Philately.*

Collectors Club, Inc., F. Burton Sellers, 22 East 35th St., New York, N. Y. 10016. Publishes *The Collectors Club Philatelist.*

Ferrary Society, Barbara Ann Lyon, Pleasant Valley, N. Y. 12569. Publishes *The Bulletin.*

Junior Philatelic Society of America, Robert J. Osterhoff, 1478 Jackson St., Dubuque, Iowa 52001. Publishes *The Philatelic Observer.*

Masonic Stamp Club of New York, Samuel Brooks, 985 Anderson Ave., Bronx, N. Y. Publishes *The Masonic Philatelist.*

National Philatelic Society, C. V. Webb, 55 Harmon Ave., Painesville, Ohio. Official organ, *National Stamp News.*

National Philatelic Society (of Great Britain), Gerald H. Simpson, 44 Fleet Street, London E. C. 4, England. Publishes *The Stamp Lover.*

Philatelic Association of Government Employees, Emanuel Toula, Box 345, Devil's Elbow, Mo. 65457. Publishes *Stampage.*

Royal Philatelic Society of Canada, Walter F. Anderson, Box 3144, Station "C," Ottawa, Ont., Canada. Publishes *The Canadian Philatelist.*

Royal Philatelic Society, London, 41 Devonshire Place, London W. 1, England. Publishes *The London Philatelist.*

Royal Philatelic Society of Victoria, G. A. F. Evans, Box 222, G. P. O., Melbourne, Australia. Publishes *Philately from Australia.*

Society of Philatelic Americans, Stewart T. Bailey, Box 266, Cincinnati, O. 45201. Publishes *S. P. A. Journal.*

REGIONAL SOCIETIES

Gastineau Philatelic Society, Jack Popejoy, 620 Seatter St., Juneau, Alaska 90081.

Arizona Philatelic Research Society, James M. Chemi, 5932 N. 14th Place, Phoenix, Ariz. 85014.

Council of Northern California Philatelic Societies, Robert J. Weims, 2209 Redwood Rd., Napa, Calif. Publishes *The Council Courier.*

Federated Philatelic Clubs of Southern California, Emily Moorefield, P. O. Box 3313, Long Beach, Calif. 90803.

San Francisco-Pacific Philatelic Society, Mrs. M. R. Ogden, 1663 30th Ave., San Francisco, Calif. 94122.

Central States Federation of Stamp Clubs, Dolores Christmas, 1654 North Bend Rd., Cincinnati, Ohio 45224. Publishes *Area Airings.*

Associated Stamp Clubs of the Chesapeake Area, Mrs. Anna D. Plant, 2022 Columbia Rd. N. W., Washington, D. C. 20009.

Confederate States Stamp Association, Edward F. Williams, Box 17659, Memphis, Tenn. 38117. Publishes *The Dixie Philatelist.*

Connecticut Philatelic Society, Betty Maukauskas, 33 Burnside Ave., Apt. 4B, East Hartford, Conn. 06108. Publishes *C. P. S. News.*

Florida Federation of Stamp Clubs, Kenneth R. Laurence, 980 N. E. 32nd St., North Miami, Fla. 33163. Publishes *The Florida Philatelist.*

Illinois Federation of Stamp Clubs, Fred H. Boedow, 5065 W. Wolcott Ave., Chicago, Ill. 60640. Publishes *News.*

Northern Indiana Philatelic Society, Foster H. Malone, 513 W. 13th St., Mishawaka, Ind. Publishes *Stampazino.*

Federation of Iowa Stamp Clubs, Wilbur A. Field, 1312 21st Ave. S. E., Cedar Rapids, Iowa 52404.

Maine Philatelic Society, Victor A. Schlich, 75 Berwick, South Portland, Maine 04106.

Midwest Philatelic Society, Adolph Pearson, 1010 Baltimore Ave., Kansas City, Mo. Publishes *The Bulletin.*

Peninsular State Philatelic Society, Marvin Preston, 640 W. Woodland, Ferndale, Mich. Publishes *The Peninsular Philatelist.*

North Jersey Federated Stamp Clubs, Inc., Mrs. Elizabeth Kreegar, 125 Wood Ave., Linden, N. J. Publishes *The North Jersey Philatelist.*

Association of South Jersey Stamp Clubs, Inc., Helen Rocco, 405 North 8th St., Vineland, N. J. 08360. Publishes *SOJEX Bulletin.*

New Mexico Philatelic Association, Mrs. Joyce Frank, Box 666, Sante Fe, New Mexico 87501. Publishes *The New Mexico Philatelist.*

Federation of Central New York Philatelic Societies, Cleon A. Morey, R. F. D. 1, Verona, N. Y. 13478. Publishes *Federation Directory.*

Nassau-Suffolk Philatelic Alliance, Mrs. Margaret O'Rourke, P. O. Box 192, Hempstead, N. Y. 11551.

Oregon Stamp Society, Mrs. O. W. Kortge, P. O. Box 3494, Portland, Ore. 97208. Publishes *The Album Page.*

North Eastern Pennsylvania Philatelic Society, Marjorie R. Travis, R. F. D. 1, Falls, Pa.

Southeastern Pennsylvania and Delaware Associated Clubs, H. Frederick Vopper, 2019 Westmoreland St., Philadelphia, Pa. 19134.

Sociedad Filatélica de Puerto Rico, Carlos Mantaras, Box 607, Rio Piedras, Puerto Rico. Publishes *Puerto Rico Filatélico.*

Rhode Island Philatelic Society, Arthur B. Jackson, 58 Dean Ave., Johnston, R. I. 02919.

Silver State Stamp Club, Mrs. Margaret E. Jueneman, 1950 Wilder, Reno, Nevada.

Texas Philatelic Association, Robert D. Zehr, Sr., 927 Hammond Ave., San Antonio, Texas 78210. Publishes *The Texas Philatelist.*

Trans-Mississippi Philatelic Society, Ruth Miller, P. O. Box 24, Allison, Iowa 50602. Official organ, *Mekeel's Weekly Stamp News.*

Utah Philatelic Society, Inc., Pat Christenbury, 1517 Harvard Ave., Salt Lake City, Utah.

Vermont Philatelic Society, Lloyd T. Hayward, 67 Liberty St., Montpelier, Vt. 05607. Publishes *The Vermont Philatelist.*

Collectors Club of Washington, D. C., Donald B. Brenke, 1101 Massachusetts Ave. N. W., Apt. 410, Washington, D. C. 20005. Publishes *The Bulletin.*

Washington State Philatelic Society, Inc., Rose Nortum, 7036 15th Ave. N. E., Seattle, Wash. Publishes *The Bulletin.*

CHAPTER 3

Foreign Currency Exchange

EXCHANGE RATES in U.S. dollars are quoted here *
by courtesy of Deak & Co. (Times Square), Inc.,
New York. An asterisk beside the country name
indicates a wider than normal fluctuation between
the Official and Free market rates. The changes
occur mostly in the Free rates, which are more real-
istic than the Official because they are tied directly
to supply and demand. The Official rates are sometimes deceiving as governments establish them for
certain types of payments which have to be made
through official channels in international trading.
The Free rate represents what people in and outside
a country think its currency is really worth.

These are the major changes in currencies during
the last couple of years:

Argentina and Brazil have devalued three times.
India devalued its rupee by more than 30 per cent.
Indonesia revalued, making 1,000 old rupiahs worth
1 new rupiah. This changed the official rate of about
10,000 rupiahs for $1 to 10 new rupiahs for $1.
Yugoslavia also revalued, turning 100 old dinars
into 1 new dinar.

The decimal system has been adopted by Australia and the Bahamas, which have discarded their

* As of Oct. 1, 1966.

pounds for dollars, and by Ghana, which has gone from pounds to cedis. Britain plans to embrace the decimal system by 1970.

The governments of Kenya, Uganda and Tanzania plan to break their ties to the East African (British) shilling and issue their own currencies. Kenya will act first.

Country	Currency	Official Rate	Free Rate
Abu Dhabi	1000 naye paise = 1 rupee	.21	
Afghanistan	100 pouls = 1 rupee Afghani	.022	.0135
Ajman	100 naye paise = 1 rupee	.21	
Albania *	100 qintar = 1 lek	.02	.0066
Algeria	100 centimes = 1 dinar	.204	.15
Andorra (French)	100 centimes = 1 franc	.2025	.205
Andorra (Spanish)	100 centimos = 1 peseta	.0167	.017
Angola	100 centavos = 1 escudo	.0348	.027
Antigua	100 cents = 1 BWI dollar	.588	.59
Argentina	100 centavos = 1 peso		.0044
Ascension	12 pence = 1 shilling		
	20 shillings = 1 pound	2.80	2.72
Australia	100 cents = 1 dollar	1.12	1.11
Austria	100 groschen = 1 schilling	.0385	.0396
Bahamas	100 cents = 1 dollar	.98	.98
Bahrain	1000 fils = 1 dinar	2.10	1.40
Barbados	100 cents = 1 BWI dollar	.588	.59
Belgium	100 centimes = 1 franc	.02	.0204
Bolivia	100 centavos = 1 peso	.0821	.08
Botswana	100 cents = 1 rand	1.40	1.37
Brazil	100 centavos = 1 cruzeiro		.000455
British Guiana	See Guyana		
British Honduras	100 cents = 1 dollar	.70	.58
British Solomon Is.	100 cents = 1 Australian dollar	1.12	1.11
Brunei	100 cents = 1 Malayan dollar	.33	.328
Bulgaria *	100 stotinki = 1 lev	.855	.39
Burma *	100 pyas = 1 kyat	.21	.0625
Burundi *	100 centimes = 1 franc	.02025	.006
Cambodia *	100 cents = 1 riel	.0285	.0125
Cameroun	100 centimes = 1 CFA franc	.0041	.004

* Countries with asterisks are those tending to have wider fluctuations between Official and Free market rates, and are subject to more frequent change.

Country	Currency	Official Rate	Free Rate
Canada	100 cents = 1 dollar	.925	.9325
Cape Verde	100 centavos = 1 escudo	.0348	.027
Cayman Islands	12 pence = 1 shilling		
	10 shillings = 1 pound	2.80	2.7
Central African Rep.	100 centimes = 1 CFA franc	.0041	.004
Ceylon *	100 cents = 1 rupee	.21	.1030
Chad	100 centimes = 1 CFA franc	.0041	.004
Chile	1000 milesimos = 100 centesimos		
	100 centesimos = 1 escudo	.313	.19
China	100 cents = 1 new Taiwan dollar	.025	.0247
Colombia	100 centavos = 1 peso		.0625
Congo (ex-Belgian) *	100 centimes = 1 franc	.0061	.0025
Congo (ex-French)	100 centimes = 1 CFA franc	.0041	.004
Cook Islands	12 pence = 1 shilling		
	20 shillings = 1 pound	2.80	2.20
Costa Rica	100 centimos = 1 colon	.1509	.14
Cyprus	1000 milliemes = 1 pound	2.80	2.70
Czechoslovakia *	100 haler = 1 koruna	.1389	.0385
Dahomey	100 centimes = 1 CFA franc	.0041	.004
Denmark	100 öre = 1 krone	.1447	.146
Dominica	100 cents = 1 BWI dollar	.588	.59
Dominican Republic	100 centavos = 1 peso	1.00	.90
Dubai	100 naye paise = 1 rupee	.21	
Ecuador	100 centavos = 1 sucre	.0555	.052
Ethiopia	100 cents = 1 dollar	.403	.40
Falkland Islands	12 pence = 1 shilling		
	20 shillings = 1 pound	2.80	2.20
Fiji	12 pence = 1 shilling		
	20 shillings = 1 pound	2.51	2.40
Finland	100 pennis = 1 markka	.312	.31
France	100 centimes = 1 franc	.2025	.205
Fr. Polynesia	100 centimes = 1 CFP franc	.0112	.0103
Fujeira	100 naye paise = 1 rupee	.21	
Gabon	100 centimes = 1 CFA franc	.0041	.004
Gambia	12 pence = 1 shilling		
	20 shillings = 1 pound	2.80	2.70
Germany, Democratic Republic *	100 pfennigs = 1 ostmark	.45	.11
Germany, Federal Republic	100 pfennigs = 1 deutsche mark	.25	.2515
Ghana *	100 pesewas = 1 cedi	1.16	.45

* Countries with asterisks are those tending to have wider fluctuations between Official and Free market rates, and are subject to more frequent change.

Country	Currency	Official Rate	Free Rate
Gibraltar	12 pence = 1 shilling		
	20 shillings = 1 pound	2.80	2.79
Gilbert and Ellice Islands	100 cents = 1 Australian dollar	1.12	1.12
Great Britain	12 pence = 1 shilling		
	20 shillings = 1 pound	2.80	2.82
Greece	100 lepta = 1 drachma	.033	.033
Greenland	100 öre = 1 Danish krone	.1447	.146
Grenada	100 cents = 1 BWI dollar	.588	.59
Guatemala	100 centavos = 1 quetzal	1.00	.92
Guinea *	100 centimes = 1 franc	.0041	.00134
Guyana	100 cents = 1 BWI dollar	.588	.59
Haiti	100 centimes = 1 gourde	.20	.19
Honduras	100 centavos = 1 lempira	.50	.49
Hong Kong	100 cents = 1 dollar	.175	.179
Hungary *	100 filler = 1 forint	.0852	.028
Iceland	100 aurar = 1 krona	.02325	.023
Ifni	100 centimos = 1 peseta	.0167	.017
India	100 paise = 1 rupee	.133	.10
Indonesia *	100 sen = 1 rupiah	.10	.01
Iran	See Persia		
Iraq	1000 fils = 1 dinar	2.80	2.56
Ireland	12 pence = 1 shilling		
	20 shillings = 1 pound	2.80	2.82
Israel	100 agorot = 1 pound	.333	.33
Italy	100 centesimi = 1 lira	.00161	.00162
Ivory Coast	100 centimes = 1 CFA franc	.0041	.004
Jamaica	12 pence = 1 shilling		
	20 shillings = 1 pound	2.80	2.70
Japan	100 sen = 1 yen	.00278	.00267
Jordan	1000 fils = 1 dinar	2.80	2.79
Jugoslavia	100 paras = 1 dinar	.08	.08
Kenya	12 cents = 1 shilling	.14	.13
Korea (South)	100 chon = 1 won	.0037	.0035
Kuwait	1000 fils = 1 dinar	2.80	2.79
Laos *	100 cents = 1 kip	.0042	.002
Lebanon	100 centimes = 1 piaster		
	100 piasters = 1 pound		.33
Lesotho (Basutoland)	100 cents = 1 rand	1.40	1.37
Liberia	100 cents = 1 dollar	1.00	1.00
Libia	1000 milliemes = 1 pound	2.80	2.45

* Countries with asterisks are those tending to have wider fluctuations between Official and Free market rates, and are subject to more frequent change.

Country	Currency	Official Rate	Free Rate
Liechtenstein	100 rappen = 1 franc		.233
Luxembourg	100 centimes = 1 franc	.020	.0204
Macao	100 avos = 1 pataca	.21	.18
Madagascar (Malagasy Republic)	100 centimes = 1 franc	.0041	.004
Malawi	12 pence = 1 shilling		
	20 shillings = 1 pound	2.80	2.79
Malaysia	100 sen (cents) = 1 dollar	.33	.328
Maldive Islands	100 larees = 1 India rupee	.133	.10
Mali	100 centimes = 1 CFA franc	.0041	.004
Malta	12 pence = 1 shilling		
	20 shillings = 1 pound	2.80	2.79
Mauritania	100 centimes = 1 CFA franc	.0041	.004
Mauritius	100 cents = 1 rupee	.21	.13
Mexico	100 centavos = 1 peso	.08	.08
Monaco	100 centimes = 1 franc	.2025	.205
Montserrat	100 cents = 1 BWI dollar	.588	.59
Morocco	100 francs = I dirham	.198	.165
Mozambique	100 centavos = 1 escudo	.0348	.027
Muscat	100 naye paise = 1 rupee	.133	.10
Nauru	100 cents = 1 Australian dollar	1.12	1.12
Nepal	100 paise = 1 rupee	.132	.11
Netherlands	100 cents = 1 guilder	.277	.278
Netherlands Antilles	100 cents = 1 guilder	.53	.53
New Caledonia	100 centimes = 1 CFP franc	.0112	.0103
New Hebrides (Br. & Fr.)	100 centimes = 1 CFP franc	.0112	.0103
New Zealand	12 pence = 1 shilling		
	20 shillings = 1 pound	2.80	2.15
Nicaragua	100 centavos = 1 cordoba	.1429	.14
Niger	100 centimes = 1 CFA franc	.0041	.004
Nigeria	12 pence = 1 shilling		
	20 shillings = 1 pound	2.80	2.77
Norfolk Island	100 cents = 1 dollar	1.12	1.11
Norway	100 öre = 1 krone	.14	.141
Pakistan	100 paisa = 1 rupee	.21	.1325
Panama	100 centesimos = 1 balboa	1.00	.90
Papua & New Guinea	100 cents = 1 Australian dollar	1.12	1.11
Paraguay	100 centimos = 1 guarani		.0072
Persia	100 dinars = 1 rial	.013	.0125
Peru	100 centavos = 1 sol		.0375
Philippines	100 centavos = 1 peso		.26
Pitcairn Island	12 pence = 1 shilling		
	20 shillings = 1 pound	2.80	2.50

Country	Currency	Official Rate	Free Rate
Poland *	100 groszy = 1 zloty	.25	.012
Portugal	100 centavos = 1 escudo	.0348	.036
Qatar	100 naye paise = 1 rupee	.21	
Réunion	100 centimes = 1 CFA franc	.0041	.004
Rhodesia	12 pence = 1 shilling		
	20 shillings = 1 pound	2.80	2.70
Romania *	100 bani = 1 lei	.167	.047
Russia *	100 kopecks = 1 ruble	1.111	.45
Rwanda *	100 centimes = 1 franc	.020	.006
Ryukyu Islands	100 cents = 1 US dollar	1.00	1.00
St. Helena	12 pence = 1 shilling		
	20 shillings = 1 pound	2.80	2.00
St. Kitts-Nevis	100 cents = 1 BWI dollar	.588	.59
St. Lucia	100 cents = 1 BWI dollar	.588	.59
St. Pierre & Miquelon	100 centimes = 1 CFA franc	.0041	.004
St. Thomas & Prince Islands	100 centavos = 1 escudo	.0348	.027
St. Vincent	100 cents = 1 BWI dollar	.588	.59
Salvador	100 centavos = 1 colon	.40	.36
Samoa	12 pence = 1 shilling		
	20 shillings = 1 pound	1.40	.95
San Marino	100 centesimi = 1 lira	.00161	.00162
Saudi Arabia	20 piasters = 1 riyal	.222	.225
Senegal	100 centimes = 1 CFA franc	.0041	.004
Seychelles	100 cents = 1 rupee	.21	.13
Sharjah	100 naye paise = 1 rupee	.21	
Siam (Thailand)	100 satangs = 1 baht	.048	.0478
Sierra Leone	100 cents = 1 leone	1.40	1.36
Singapore	100 cents = 1 Malayan dollar	.33	.328
Somalia	100 centesimi = 1 somalo	.14	.14
Somali Coast	100 centimes = 1 franc	.00404	.0047
South Africa	100 cents = 1 rand	1.40	1.37
South-West Africa	100 cents = 1 rand	1.40	1.37
Spain	100 centimos = 1 peseta	.0167	.017
Sudan	100 piasters = 1 pound	2.87	2.00
Surinam	100 cents = 1 guilder	.53	.53
Swaziland	100 cents = 1 rand	1.40	1.37
Sweden	100 öre = 1 krona	.193	.195
Switzerland	100 rappen = 1 franc		.233
Syria	100 centimes = 1 piaster		
	100 piasters = 1 pound		.27
Tanzania	100 cents = 1 shilling	.14	.13

* Countries with asterisks are those tending to have wider fluctuations between Official and Free market rates, and are subject to more frequent change.

Country	Currency	Official Rate	Free Rate
Thailand	*See* Siam		
Timor	100 centavos = 1 escudo	.0348	.027
Togo	100 centimes = 1 CFA franc	.0041	.004
Tonga	12 pence = 1 shilling		
	20 shillings = 1 pound	2.24	1.95
Trinidad & Tobago	100 cents = 1 BWI dollar	.588	.59
Tunisia *	100 milliemes = 1 dinar	2.38	.92
Turkey	100 kurus = 1 lira	.111	.089
Turks & Caicos Islands	12 pence = 1 shilling		
	20 shillings = 1 pound	2.80	2.79
Uganda	100 cents = 1 shilling	.14	.136
Umm al Qiwain	100 naye paise = 1 rupee	.21	
United Arab Republic *	1000 milliemes = 1 pound	2.30	1.33
Upper Volta	100 centimes = 1 CFA franc	.0041	.004
Uruguay	1000 milésimos = 1 peso		.015
Venezuela	100 centimos = 1 bolívar		.222
Viet Nam *	100 cents = 1 piaster	.0085	.00645
Virgin Islands (British)	100 cents = 1 US dollar	1.00	1.00
Wallis & Futuna Islands	100 centimes = 1 CFP franc	.0112	.0103
Zambia	12 pence = 1 shilling		
	20 shillings = 1 pound	2.80	2.70

* Countries with asterisks are those tending to have wider fluctuations between Official and Free market rates, and are subject to more frequent change.

CHAPTER 4

Magazines Around the World

SPEAKING IN many tongues, the philatelic press embraces hundreds of magazines and newspapers which pour into the mails at regular intervals in scores of countries.

Some entertain, some report gossip, some give market tips, some print serious articles by stamp students, many cover the latest new issues, and most of them carry dealers' advertisements. They all breathe life into the hobby and probably do more to keep it flourishing than any other factor, including clubs and exhibitions.

You the stamp collector cannot possibly read all of this mass of philatelic literature. But, by following a few periodicals, you can steadily increase your knowledge of the fine points of philately, and you will inevitably add to your enjoyment of the great paper chase.

The following selective list offers some of the better-known and more popular periodicals.

Austria-Philatelist, Verlag Adolf Kosel, Hebragasse 9, Vienna IX, Austria. Monthly; German; $3.50 a year.

Australian Stamp Monthly, Horticultural Press, 8 Orr St., Melbourne, Victoria, Australia. Monthly; $2.60 a year.

Balasse Magazine, 45 Rue du Midi, Brussels, Belgium. Bimonthly; French; $2 a year.

Berner Briefmarken-Zeitung, Zumstein & Cie, Postfach 2585, 3001 Bern, Switzerland. Monthly; German and French; $2.60 a year. Includes Zumstein Katalog supplement.

Canadian Philatelist, Royal Philatelic Society of Canada, 516 Kenwood Ave., Ottawa 13, Canada. Bimonthly.

Il Collezionista, Via Zuretti 25, Milan, Italy. Weekly; Italian; $12 a year.

L'Exchangiste Universel, 8 Rue Saint-Marc, Paris IIe, France. Monthly; French; $2.60 a year.

L'Echo de la Timbrologie, 37 Rue des Jacobins, Amiens, France. Monthly; French; $3 a year.

Frimaerkesamleren, The Danish Stamp Collector, Magnoliavej 2 st. th., Copenhagen, (Valby), Denmark. Monthly; Danish; $3.50 a year.

Gibbons Stamp Monthly, Stanley Gibbons, Ltd., 391 Strand, London W.C. 2, England. Monthly; $2.25 a year surface mail; $5.60 a year airmail.

India's Stamp Journal, Standard Bldg., Hornby Rd., Bombay, India. Monthly; $2 a year.

Kitte Shumi, Kitte Bunka Philatelic Society, 3-3600 Mejiro, Toshima-ku, Tokyo, Japan. Monthly; Japanese; $2.50 a year.

Linn's Weekly Stamp News, P.O. Box 29, Sidney, Ohio 45365. Weekly; $3.50 a year.

Madrid Filatélico, Casa M. Galvez, Puerta del Sol 4, Madrid 14, Spain. Monthly; Spanish; $2 a year.

Mekeel's Weekly Stamp News, P.O. Box 1660, Portland, Maine 04104. Weekly; $1.50 a year.

Michel Rundschau, Verlag des Schwaneberger Album, Eugen Berlin GmbH., Landsberger Strasse 20,

8 Munich 12, Germany. Monthly; German; $2.50 a year.

Le Monde des Philatélistes, 5 Rue des Italiens, Paris IXe, France. Monthly; French; $3.20 a year; $7.20 airmail.

Norsk Filatelistisk Tiddsskrift, Norwegian Philatelic League, P.O. Box 49, Minde, Bergen, Norway. Ten issues a year; Norwegian; $3.

Philatelic Journal of India, Philatelic Society of India, 29 Marine Lines, Fort, Bombay 1, India. Monthly; $2.95 a year.

Philatelic Magazine, Harris Publications, Ltd., 27 Maiden Lane, London W.C. 2, England. Semimonthly; $4 a year.

The Philatelist, Robson, Lowe, Ltd., 50 Pall Mall, London S.W. 1, England. Monthly; $5 a year; $8 airmail.

Philately, British Philatelic Assn., 446 Strand, London W.C. 2, England. Monthly; $1.40 a year.

Philately from Australia, Royal Philatelic Society of Victoria, Box 222, G.P.O. Melbourne, Australia. Quarterly; $3 a year.

Philippines Journal of Philately, Postal Information Office, Bureau of Posts, Manila, Philippines. Bimonthly; $2 a year.

Die Sammler-Lupe, 4152 Kempen-Niederrhein, Postfach 60, Germany. Semimonthly; German; $4.80 a year.

Schweizer Briefmarken-Zeitung, Buri & Cie, Burenstrasse 1, Bern, Switzerland. Monthly; German and French; 40 cents a copy.

Scott's Monthly Stamp Journal, Portland Place, Boulder, Colorado 80302. Monthly; $4 a year; Canada, $4.50; foreign, $5.

Stamp Collecting, 42 Maiden Lane, London W.C. 2, England. Weekly; $7 a year.

Stamp Magazine, Link House Publications, Ltd., Dingwall Ave., Croydon, Surrey, England. Monthly; $4.30 a year; $12.60 airmail.

Stamp News, Review Publications, Sterling St., Dubbo, N.S.W., Australia. Monthly; $2 a year.

Stamps, H. L. Lindquist Publications, Inc., 153 Waverly Place, New York, N. Y. 10014, Weekly; $3.90 a year.

Svenska Filatelistisk Tidskrift, Philatelic Society of Sweden, Lidnersplan 10, Stockholm K, Sweden. Ten issues a year; Swedish; $2.50 a year.

Western Stamp Collector, P.O. Box 10, Albany, Oregon 97321. Semiweekly; $2.50 a year.

CHAPTER 5

The Road to Ribbons and Medals
or How to Prepare
Your Stamps for Exhibition

IN SERIOUS COLLECTING, you eventually reach the point of wondering whether you and your stamps are ready to exhibit. Philatelic maturity is said to begin when you make your first club presentation. It develops as you go on to enter interclub competitions, then local, national, and finally, international exhibitions.

Hundreds of local shows are held throughout the United States and the rest of the world every year. This is the ideal arena for preliminary sparring. Such exhibitions help to tell the public of the pleasures of stamp collecting and enable collectors in the area to test the reactions to their displays in preparation for more important national and international events.

The rules for most exhibitions, whether local, intraclub or national, are usually based on those established for international exhibitions. To put the exhibits into a proper system, classifications must

be set up for every exhibition, regardless of size (general classifications for international, national and local exhibitions are given at the end of this section). These classifications depend on the scope of the exhibition, and in local exhibitions they are often modified to suit the types of collections found within the area.

A national stamp exhibition may have an underlying theme around which the exhibits are built, or it may be of a general nature. Usually collectors are invited to display parts of their collections, sometimes for prize awards, but often merely for certificates of participation. The object is to show the public and other collectors what to look for and aim at in the country or group concerned. Most philatelists consider it an honor to be asked to exhibit even though the reward may be intangible. INTERPEX, which is held in New York City each year, and STAMPEX, held in London, are examples of excellent, well-run national exhibitions.

International stamp exhibitions take place once or more often every year throughout the world. It is a general rule, however, that no one country should hold an international exhibit more often than once every ten years. The great international exhibitions held in the United States took place in 1913, 1926, 1936, 1947, 1956, and 1966.

These international exhibitions treat the public and collectors to a view of the finest examples of philatelic collections in the world. Much can be learned by attending an international show and studying the exhibits. This can be an eye-opening experience, and no collector should miss it.

Beside the usual classifications, international and national exhibitions may also have two other groups: (1) noncompetitive collections which are entered

in the various sections but do not compete for awards; (2) championship collections which have received high awards at previous exhibitions of the same scope. The second of these groups competes only with other collections of the same type for a championship trophy, but not for any other awards. First, second and third prizes are usually awarded within each classification of each category, with a grand prize being given for the best of all the exhibits.

Awards in any exhibition are based on the decision of judges, the number of judges depending on the size of the exhibition. In local exhibitions, three are usually the minimum, while international exhibitions are judged by juries composed of up to thirty or more eminent philatelists from numerous countries.

Whether your exhibit is a highly specialized or research collection, a general one, or one of topical interest, there are five categories which most judges will use in determining its merits. These are:

(1) Presentation. The manner in which the collector presents his material must be clear and simple. It must be disciplined to create an initial impression to the viewer so that the person looking at the presentation for the first time will be interested enough to follow through and observe all details of the exhibit. Use a title page to tell the judges what you are trying to show with your stamps. If you are exhibiting a study of the Kicking Mule cancellation, tell that with your title page. Proper headings will carry the continuity of your exhibit.

Since it is impossible to show your complete collection, it is often better to specialize the pages you are presenting by developing a certain phase, period or specific category than by showing a few pages

selected at random from your collection, which may cover a wider scope.

The appearance of your exhibit as a whole, and that of each individual page, should be made as attractive as possible. The best way to plan your pages is to gather all the material for each page and lay it out on the page, experimenting with different layouts until you determine the most suitable one. This will prevent a haphazard appearance and assure uniformity for your exhibit.

With topical collections particularly, it is important to include a write-up. A page of stamps on Renaissance art may be interesting to you, but without write-ups and explanations as to why it is interesting and important, it is seldom more than just another page to a viewer. Only pertinent information should be included in the write-up. The judge has many exhibits to study and does not have time or inclination to wade through a lot of unnecessary verbiage. Some think the hand-penned write-up is best. Others believe that if the collector has feeble or sloppy penmanship, a neat, typewritten page is better. A third way is to entrust the inscribing to an experienced professional who will probably do a better job than either you or your typewriter.

The pages of your exhibit can often be brightened by making judicious use of attention-getting pictures, maps, diagrams, etc. Any outside material, however, should add something of value to your pages and not distract from the stamps themselves.

(2) Philatelic Knowledge and Research. Research can be either original or a gathering and distillation of previously recorded knowledge about your stamps. The research must present the flow of the investigator's thought concerning his analysis and findings.

The mechanical processes involved in the use of paper and printing create broad fields such as plating. Other rich areas for research include postal history, early covers, perforation studies of one issue, color varieties, the story behind the issuance of the stamp, watermarks, differences in use of the issue, and many, many more. To present the complete story is the important thing.

(3) **Condition.** Condition is the measure of the stamps, covers, etc., to be shown. As most exhibits these days are enclosed in glass-covered frames, the condition of the gum or back surfaces is secondary. You should always use the best material that can be obtained. Valuable judging points will be lost if you present a torn cover or heavily canceled stamps.

(4) **Rarity.** The monetary value of the material is far from the overriding factor of judging. For example, the 24-cent U.S. airmail invert cataloguing $18,500 would be many times the value of a collection of a less popular country, such as Ethiopia. Yet interest and rarity can exist in high degree in stamps of an unpopular country.

(5) **Completeness.** "Completeness" is a deceptive word and can mean different things to different collectors. This aspect is sometimes difficult to judge. Catalogue listings are usually a criterion for judging completeness. If an exhibitor's presentation has what appear to be obvious holes, as indicated by catalogue listings, the presentation is not really ready for exhibition. On the other hand, if the exhibitor's objective is to limit the presentation, he may have many "holes." Often it is possible to prevent criticism in this area by stating that your pages are selected from a collection; then the judges should look for representativeness. The material presented must be

representative, and it must contain significant items that relate to one another in a manner that tells the story in simple, logical order.

Any worthwhile exhibit takes time. Collecting stamps and covers for this purpose takes a considerable amount of research and effort. Assembling the facts and arranging the material in a manner that pleases the eye and challenges the viewer is not easy. But it enables you, the exhibitor, to know your own material better and to become more expert in your field.

Don't expect to be able to enter your stamps and win an award the first time. Good exhibiting, like everything else, comes through experience. Don't be discouraged if you fail to win a ribbon immediately. When the judging is over, think about your presentation in a positive manner and ask yourself where you could have done better. Ask one of the judges for criticism. He will be pleased that you are interested enough in his judgment to accept his criticism positively and creatively.

Think through the five judging categories and use them as the basis for assembling your material. Then you will have a good chance of winning an award at the next exhibition you enter.

Classification of an International Exhibition

Section I: National

1. General collections
2. Postage issues, 19th century
3. Postage issues, 20th century
4. Local & private-post stamps
5. Other special-function stamps
6. Envelopes, wrappers, postal cards
7. Revenue stamps
8. Postal history
9. Essays, proofs, specimen stamps
10. Possessions & administrative stamps
11. Any not classified above

Section II: British Empire
Section III: Europe & Colonies (except British Empire)
Section IV: Latin America
Section V: Africa, Asia & Others

Sections II to V are broken down into subgroups similar to those in Section I, but less specialized.

Section VI: Airmail

1. General
2. Specialized
3. Semiofficial
4. Special flights
5. Rocket, missile & space-age material
6. Postal stationery

Section VII: Topical
Section VIII: Junior

1. National
2. Other countries
3. Topical

Section IX: Philatelic Literature

1. Handbooks
2. Brochures
3. Study papers
4. Periodicals
5. Catalogues
6. All others

Sometimes a Section X is added for General Collections, but the current trend is that more and more collectors are exhibiting parts of their collections covering one or two countries.

Classification of a National Exhibit

Here the outline is not quite as extensive as in the international exhibitions.

Section I: National Class, including Possessions
1. 19th century
2. 20th century
3. Special groups

Section II: British Empire

Section III: Foreign, except British Empire

Section IV: General Collections (all material not in Sections I–III).

The three subclassifications of Section I are repeated for Sections II–IV.

Classification of a Local Exhibition

Some local exhibitions have almost as many sections as a national show, but it is becoming increasingly popular to have only four.

Section I: National

Section II: Other Countries

Section III: Topical

Section IV: Junior

Subclassifications are few, if any.

CHAPTER 6

First Issues of the World

GREAT BRITAIN issued its Penny Black, the world's
first postage stamp, in 1840. Since then scarcely a
year has gone by without another country's releasing
its first stamps. Students of postal history and collectors of stamp centenary issues or first issues
should find interest in this listing. It gives in chronological order—from 1840 through 1966—the first
issues of the world with Scott Catalogue number,
denomination, color, design subject, and method of
printing.

Until Sierra Leone's 6 pence of September 21,
1859, appeared with perforation 14 by De La Rue,
all first issues had been imperforate. The seven other
first issues of 1859 are imperforate. From 1860
onward, all in this list are perforated except those
few described otherwise.

First issues of more than one denomination, such
as the 1847 U.S. 5c and 10c, are represented in
this list by the low value.

Great Britain

1840
Great Britain No. 1, 1 penny black, Queen Victoria, engraved.

1843
Brazil No. 1, 30 reis black, Numeral, engraved.
Switzerland No. 1L1, 4 rappen black of Zurich, Numeral,
lithographed.

Switzerland—Zurich

Bavaria

1847

Mauritius No. 1, 1 penny orange, Queen Victoria, engraved.

United States No. 1, 5 cents red brown, Benjamin Franklin, engraved.

1849

Bavaria No. 1, 1 kreuzer black, Numeral, typographed.

Belgium No. 1, 10 centimes brown, King Leopold I, engraved.

France No. 1, 10 centimes bister, Ceres, typographed.

Lombardy-Venetia

1850

Austria No. 1, 1 kreuzer yellow, Coat of Arms, typographed.

British Guiana No. 2, 2 cents orange, Numeral and Name, typeset.

Hanover No. 1, 1 gute groschen gray blue, Coat of Arms, typographed.

Lombardy-Venetia No. 1, 5 centesimi buff, Coat of Arms, typographed.

New South Wales No. 1, 1 penny red, Seal of Colony, engraved.

Prussia No. 2, 6 pfennigs red orange, King Frederick William IV, engraved.

Saxony No. 1, 3 pfennigs red, Numeral, typographed.

Schleswig-Holstein No. 1, 1 schilling dull blue and bluish green, Coat of Arms, typographed and embossed.

Spain No. 1, 6 cuartos black, Queen Isabella II, lithographed.

Victoria No. 1, 1 penny dull red, Queen Victoria, lithographed.

Saxony

1851

Baden No. 1, 1 kreuzer black on dark buff, Numeral, typographed.

Canada No. 1, 3 pence red, Beaver, engraved.

Denmark No. 1, 2 rigsbank skillings blue, Numeral, typographed.

Hawaii No. 1, 2 cents blue, Numeral, typeset.

New Brunswick No. 1, 3 pence red, Crown of Great Britain, engraved.

Nova Scotia No. 1, 1 penny red brown, Queen Victoria, engraved.

Sardinia No. 1, 5 centesimi gray black, King Victor Emmanuel II, lithographed.

Denmark

Trinidad No. 2, 1 penny purple brown, Britannia, engraved.

Tuscany No. 2, 1 soldo ocher, Lion of Tuscany, typographed.

Wurttemberg No. 1, 1 kreuzer black on buff, Numeral, typographed.

Tuscany

Württemberg

Barbados

1852

Barbados No. 1, ½ penny deep green, Britannia, engraved.

Brunswick No. 1, 1 silbergroschen rose, Leaping Saxon Horse, typographed.

Luxembourg No. 1, 10 centimes gray black, Grand Duke William III, engraved.

Netherlands No. 1, 5 cents blue, King William III, engraved.

Oldenburg No. 1, 1/30 thaler black on blue, Numeral, lithographed.

Parma No. 1, 5 centesimi black on yellow, Crown and Fleur-de-lis, typographed.

Réunion No. 1, 15 centimes black on blue, Numeral and Name, typographed.

Roman States No. 1, ½ bajocco black on dull violet, Papal Arms, typographed.

Thurn and Taxis No. 1, ¼ silbergroschen black on red brown, Numeral, typographed.

Denmark

Thurn and Taxis

1853

Cape of Good Hope No. 1, 1 penny red, "Hope" Seated, engraved.

Cape of Good Hope

Chile No. 1, 5 centavos brown red, Christopher Columbus, engraved.

Tasmania No. 1, 1 penny blue, Queen Victoria, engraved.

1854

India No. 1, ½ anna red, Queen Victoria, lithographed.

Philippines No. 1, 5 cuartos orange, Queen Isabella II, engraved.

Western Australia No. 1, 1 penny black, Swan, engraved.

1855

Bremen No. 1, 3 grote black on blue, Coat of Arms, lithographed.

Bremen

Cuba No. 1, ½ real plata blue green, Queen Isabella II, typographed.

Danish West Indies No. 1, 3 cents dark carmine, Coat of Arms, typographed.

New Zealand No. 1, 1 penny dull carmine, Queen Victoria, engraved.

Norway No. 1, 4 skillings blue, Coat of Arms, typographed.

Portugal No. 1, 5 reis orange brown, Queen Maria II, typographed and embossed.

South Australia No. 2, 2 pence dull carmine, Queen Victoria, engraved.

Sweden No. 1, 3 skillings banco blue green, Coat of Arms, typographed.

South Australia

Sweden

Finland

1856

Finland No. 1, 5 kopecks blue, Coat of Arms, typographed.

Mexico No. 1, ½ real blue, Miguel Hidalgo y Costilla, engraved.

St. Helena No. 1, 6 pence blue, Queen Victoria, engraved.

St. Helena

Uruguay No. 1, 60 centavos blue, El Sol de Mayo, lithographed.

1857
Ceylon No. 1, 1 pence blue, Queen Victoria, engraved.
Natal No. 1, 3 pence black on rose, Crown and V.R., embossed.
Newfoundland No. 1, 1 penny brown violet, Crown of Great Britain, engraved.
Peru No. 1, 1 real blue, Sail and Steamship, engraved.
Russia No. 1, 10 kopecks brown and blue, Coat of Arms, typographed.

Uruguay

1858
Argentina No. 1, 5 centavos red, Confederation Symbols, lithographed.
Romania No. 1, 27 parale black on rose, Arms of Moldavia, handstamped.
Two Sicilies No. 1, ½ grano pale lake, Coat of Arms, engraved.

1859
Bahamas No. 1, 1 penny pale lake, Queen Victoria, engraved.
Colombia No. 1, 2½ centavos green, Coat of Arms, lithographed.

Romania

Hamburg No. 1, ½ schilling black, Numeral, typographed.
Ionian Islands No. 1, ½ penny orange, Queen Victoria, engraved.
New Caledonia No. 1, 10 centimes black, Napoleon III, lithographed.
Romagna No. 1, ½ bajocco black on straw, Value and Name, typographed.
Sierra Leone No. 1, 6 pence dull violet, Queen Victoria, typographed.
Venezuela No. 1, ½ real orange, Coat of Arms, lithographed.

Romagna

1860
British Columbia and Vancouver Island No. 1, 2½ pence dull rose, Queen Victoria, typographed, imperforate.
Jamaica No. 1, 1 penny blue, Queen Victoria, typographed.
Liberia No. 1, 6 cents red, Coat of Arms, lithographed.
Malta No. 2, ½ penny buff on bluish, Queen Victoria, typographed.
Poland No. 1, 10 kopecks blue and rose, Coat of Arms, typographed.

Malta

Queensland No. 1, 1 penny deep rose, Queen Victoria, engraved, imperforate.

St. Lucia No. 1, 1 penny rose red, Queen Victoria, engraved.

1861

Greece No. 1, 1 lepton chocolate, Hermes, typographed, imperforate.

Grenada No. 1, 1 penny green, Queen Victoria, engraved.

Nevis No. 1, 1 penny lake rose, Medicinal Spring, engraved.

Prince Edward Island No. 1, 2 pence dull rose, Queen Victoria, typographed.

St. Vincent No. 1, 1 penny rose, Queen Victoria, engraved.

1862

Antigua No. 1, 6 pence blue green, Queen Victoria, engraved.

Hong Kong No. 1, 2 cents pale brown, Queen Victoria, typographed.

Italy No. 17, 10 centesimi bister, King Victor Emmanuel II, typographed and embossed.

Mecklenburg-Schwerin No. 1, 4¼ schillings red, Coat of Arms, typographed, imperforate.

Nicaragua No. 1, 2 centavos dark blue, Liberty Cap on Mountain Peak, engraved.

1863

Costa Rica No. 1, ½ real blue, Coat of Arms, engraved.

Turkey No. 1, 20 paras yellow, Tughra, lithographed, imperforate.

1864

Dutch Indies No. 1, 10 cents lake, King William III, engraved, imperforate.

Mecklenburg-Strelitz No. 1, ¼ silbergroschen orange, Coat of Arms, typographed and embossed, rouletted.

1865

Bermuda No. 1, 1 penny dull blue, Queen Victoria, typographed.

British Honduras No. 1, 1 penny blue, Queen Victoria, typographed.

Dominican Republic No. 1, ½ real black on rose, Coat of Arms, typographed, imperforate.

Ecuador No. 1, 1 real yellow, Coat of Arms, typographed, imperforate.

Honduras No. 1, 2 reales green, Coat of Arms, lithographed, imperforate.

Shanghai No. 1, 2 candareens black, Dragon, typographed, imperforate.

1866

Bergedorf No. 1, ½ schilling black on pale blue, Coat of Arms, lithographed, imperforate.
Egypt No. 1, 5 paras, slate green, lithographed.
Serbia No. 1, 1 para green on violet rose, Coat of Arms, typographed, imperforate.
Virgin Islands No. 1, 1 penny green, Virgin and Lamps, lithographed.

Bergedorf

1867

Heligoland No. 1, ½ schilling blue, green and rose, Queen Victoria, typographed and embossed, rouletted.
Salvador No. 1, ½ real blue, San Miguel Volcano, engraved.
Straits Settlements No. 1, 1½ pence blue, Queen Victoria, typographed.
Turks Islands No. 1, 1 penny rose, Queen Victoria, engraved.

1868

Azores No. 1, 5 reis black, King Luiz, typographed and embossed, imperforate.
Bolivia No. 1, 5 centavos blue, Condor, engraved, imperforate.
Fernando Po No. 1, 20 centimos brown, Queen Isabella II, typographed.
Madeira No. 1, 20 reis bister, King Luiz, typographed and embossed, imperforate.
North German Confederation No. 1, ¼ groschen red lilac, Numeral, typographed, rouletted.
Orange River Colony No. 3, 1 penny brown, Orange Tree, typographed.

1869

Gambia No. 1, 4 pence pale brown, Queen Victoria, embossed, imperforate.
St. Thomas and Prince Islands No. 1, 5 reis black, Portuguese Crown, typographed.
Sarawak No. 1, 3 cents brown, Sir James Brooke, lithographed.
Transvaal No. 1, 1 penny brown lake, Coat of Arms, engraved, imperforate.

1870

Afghanistan No. 2, 1 shahi black, Tiger's Head, lithographed, imperforate.

Angola No. 1, 5 reis black, Portuguese Crown, typographed.

Fiji No. 1, 1 penny black on pink, Value and Name, typeset, rouletted.

Paraguay No. 1, 1 real rose, Lion and Liberty Cap, lithographed, imperforate.

Persia No. 1, 1 shahi dull violet, Coat of Arms, typographed, imperforate.

St. Christopher No. 1, 1 penny dull rose, Queen Victoria, typographed.

1871

Guatemala No. 1, 1 centavo bister, Coat of Arms, typographed.

Hungary No. 1, 2 krajczár orange, Franz Josef I, lithographed.

Japan No. 1, 48 mon brown, Dragons, engraved, imperforate.

Portuguese India No. 1, 10 reis black, Numeral, handstamped.

Hungary

1872

German Empire No. 1, ¼ silbergroschen violet, Imperial Eagle, typographed.

1873

Curaçao (Netherlands Antilles) No. 1, 2½ cents green, King William III, typographed.

Iceland No. 1, 2 skillings ultramarine, Numeral, typographed.

Puerto Rico No. 1, 25 cents gray, King Amadeo, typographed.

Surinam No. 1, 1 cent lilac gray, King William III, typographed.

1874

Dominica No. 1, 1 penny violet, Queen Victoria, typographed.

Lagos No. 1, 1 penny lilac, Queen Victoria, typographed.

Montenegro No. 1, 2 novcic yellow, Prince Nicholas I, typographed.

1875

Gold Coast No. 1, 1 pence blue, Queen Victoria, typographed.

1876

Malaya—Johore No. 1, 2 cents brown, Queen Victoria, typographed.

Montserrat No. 1, 1 penny red, Queen Victoria, engraved.

1877

Cape Verde No. 1, 5 reis black, Portuguese Crown, typographed.

Griqualand West No. 1, 1 pence blue, "Hope," typographed.

Mozambique No. 1, 5 reis black, Portuguese Crown, typographed.

Samoa No. 1, 1 penny blue, Value and Name, lithographed.

San Marino No. 1, 2 centesimi green, Coat of Arms, typographed.

1878

China No. 1, 1 candareen green, Imperial Dragon, typographed.

Falkland Islands No. 1, 1 penny claret, Queen Victoria, engraved.

Malaya—Perak No. 1, 2 cents brown, Queen Victoria, typographed.

Malaya—Selangor No. 1, 2 cents brown, Queen Victoria, typographed.

Malaya—Sungei Ujong No. 2, 2 cents brown, Queen Victoria, typographed.

Panama No. 1, 5 centavos gray green, Coat of Arms, lithographed, imperforate.

Falkland Islands

1879

Bulgaria No. 1, 5 centimes black and yellow, Lion of Bulgaria, typographed.

Labuan No. 1, 2 cents green, Queen Victoria, engraved.

Tobago No. 1, 1 penny rose, Queen Victoria, typographed.

1880

Cyprus No. 1, ½ penny rose, Queen Victoria, engraved.

Eastern Rumelia No. 1, ½ piaster yellow green, Crescent and Star, typographed.

1881

Haiti No. 1, 1 centime vermilion, Liberty Head, typographed, imperforate.

Nepal No. 1, 1 anna ultramarine, Sripech and Crossed Khukris, typographed.

Portuguese Guinea No. 1, 5 reis black, Portuguese Crown, typographed.

1882

Bangkok No. 1, 2 cents brown, Queen Victoria, typographed.

Tahiti No. 1, 25 centimes on 35c dark violet on orange, Peace and Commerce, typographed, imperforate.

1883

North Borneo No. 1, 2 cents brown, Coat of Arms, lithographed.

Siam No. 1, 1 solot blue, King Chulalongkorn, engraved.

1884

Guadeloupe No. 1, 20 centimes on 30c brown on bister, Peace and Commerce, typographed, imperforate.

Korea No. 1, 5 mon rose, Yin Yang, typographed.

Macao No. 1, 5 reis black, Portuguese Crown, typographed.

Madagascar No. 1, 1 penny violet, Arms of Great Britain, typographed, rouletted.

Stellaland No. 1, 1 penny red, Coat of Arms, typographed.

1885

Monaco No. 1, 1 centime olive green, Prince Charles III, typographed.

St. Pierre & Miquelon No. 1, 5 centimes on 40c vermilion on straw, Peace and Commerce, typographed, imperforate.

Timor No. 1, 5 reis black, Portuguese Crown, typographed.

1886

Bechuanaland No. 1, 4 pence blue, Seal of Cape of Good Hope, typographed.

Cochin China No. 1, 5 centimes yellow, Commerce, typographed.

Congo No. 1, 5 centimes green, King Leopold II, typographed.

French Guiana No. 1, 5 centimes on 2c green, Peace and Commerce, typographed, imperforate.

Gabon No. 1, 5 centimes red, Commerce, typographed.

Gibraltar No. 1, ½ penny green, Queen Victoria, typographed.

Martinique No. 1, 5 centimes red, Commerce, typographed.

New Republic No. 1, 1 penny violet, Name and Value, handstamped.

Tonga No. 1, 1 penny carmine rose, King George I, typographed.

1887

Senegal No. 1, 5 centimes on 20c red on green, Commerce, typographed.

1888

Bechuanaland Protectorate No. 51, ½ pence vermilion, Queen Victoria, typographed.

Tunisia No. 1, 1 centime blue, Coat of Arms, typographed.

Zululand No. 1, ½ penny vermilion, Queen Victoria, typographed.

1889

Indo-China No. 1, 5 centimes on 35c deep violet on orange, Commerce, typographed.

Nossi-Bé No. 1, 25 centimes on 40c red on straw, Peace and Commerce, typographed, imperforate.

Swaziland No. 1, ½ pence gray, Coat of Arms, typographed.

1890

Diégo-Suarez No. 1, 15 centimes on 1c black on blue, Commerce, typographed.

British East Africa No. 1, ½ anna on 1 penny lilac, Queen Victoria, engraved, typographed.

Leeward Islands No. 1, ½ penny lilac and green, Queen Victoria, typographed.

Malaya—Pahang No. 1, 2 cents rose, Queen Victoria, typographed.

Rhodesia No. 2, 1 penny black, Coat of Arms, engraved.

Seychelles No. 1, 2 cents green and rose, Queen Victoria, typographed.

1891

British Central Africa No. 1, 1 penny black, Coat of Arms, engraved.

French Congo No. 1, 5 centimes on 1c black on lilac blue, Commerce, typographed.

French Morocco No. 1, 5 centimos on 5 centimes green on greenish, Peace and Commerce, typographed.

Malaya—Negri Sembilan No. 1, 2 cents rose, Queen Victoria, typographed.

1892

Bénin No. 1, 1 centime black on bluish, Commerce, typographed.

Cook Islands No. 1, 1 penny black, Value and Name, typographed.

Eritrea No. 1, 1 centesimo bronze green, Numeral, typographed.

Funchal No. 1, 5 reis yellow, King Carlos, typographed.

French India No. 1, 1 centime black on lilac blue, Navigation and Commerce, typographed.

French Polynesia No. 1, 1 centime black on lilac blue, Navigation and Commerce, typographed.

Horta No. 1, 5 reis yellow, King Carlos, typographed.

Ivory Coast No. 1, 1 centime black on lilac blue, Navigation and Commerce, typographed.

Mayotte No. 1, 1 centime black on lilac blue, Navigation and Commerce, typographed.

Mozambique Company No. 1, 5 reis black, King Luiz, embossed.

Niger Coast Protectorate No. 1, ½ pence vermilion, Queen Victoria, typographed.

Obock No. 1, 1 centime black on lilac blue, Commerce, typographed.

1893

German East Africa No. 1, 2 pesa on 3 pfennigs brown, Numeral, typographed.

1894

Ethiopia No. 1, ¼ guerche green, Menelik II, typographed.

French Sudan No. 1, 15 centimes on 75c carmine on rose, Commerce, typographed.

Portuguese Congo No. 1, 5 reis yellow, King Carlos, typographed.

Ste.-Marie de Madagascar No. 1, 1 centime black on lilac blue, Navigation and Commerce, typographed.

Somali Coast No. 1, 5 centimes green on greenish, Navigation and Commerce, typographed.

Zambézia No. 1, 5 reis yellow, King Carlos, typographed.

1895

Inhambane No. 1, 5 reis black, Coat of Arms, typographed.

Lourenço Marques No. 1, 5 reis yellow, King Carlos, typographed.

Uganda No. 1, 5 cowries black, "U G" and Value, typewritten, imperforate.

Zanzibar No. 1, ½ anna green, Queen Victoria, typographed.

1897

Cameroun No. 1, 3 pfennigs yellow brown, Numeral, typographed.

German South-West Africa No. 1, 3 pfennigs dark brown, Numeral, typographed.

Grand Comoro No. 1, 1 centime black on lilac blue, Navigation and Commerce, typographed.

Marshall Islands No. 1, 3 pfennigs dark brown, Numeral, typographed.

Sudan No. 1, 1 millieme brown, Sphinx and Pyramid, typographed.

Togo No. 1, 3 pfennigs dark brown, Numeral, typographed.

1898

Crete No. 1, 20 paras violet, handstamped, imperforate.

German New Guinea No. 1, 3 pfennigs brown, Numeral, typographed.

Nyassa No. 1, 5 reis yellow, King Carlos, typographed.

1899

Caroline Islands No. 1a, 3 pfennigs light brown, Numeral and Crown, typographed.

Dahomey No. 8, 25 centimes black on rose, Navigation and Commerce, typographed.

Guam No. 1, 1 cent deep green, Benjamin Franklin, engraved.

Mariana Islands No. 1, 2 centavos dark blue green, King Alfonso XIII, typographed.

1900

Cayman Islands No. 1, ½ penny green, Queen Victoria, typographed.

Kiauchau No. 1, 5 pfennigs on 10 pf carmine, Imperial German Eagle, typographed.

Malaya—Federated Malay States No. 1, 1 cent lilac and green, Tiger's Head, typographed.

Turks and Caicos Islands No. 1, ½ penny green, Dependency's Badge, engraved.

1901

British New Guinea No. 1, ½ penny yellow green, Lakatoi, engraved.

Southern Nigeria No. 1, ½ penny yellow green and black, Queen Victoria, typographed.

1902

Niue No. 1, 1 pence carmine, Commerce, engraved.

Spanish Guinea No. 1, 5 centimos dark green, King Alfonso XIII, typographed.

1903

Aitutaki No. 1, ½ pence green, Mt. Cook, engraved.

East Africa and Uganda Protectorates No. 1, ½ anna gray green, King Edward VII, typographed.

Elobey, Annobon and Corisco No. 1, ¼ centimo carmine, King Alfonso XIII, typographed.

Italian Somaliland No. 1, 1 besa brown, Elephant, typographed.

St. Kitts-Nevis No. 1, ½ penny green and violet, Columbus
Looking for Land, typographed.

Senegambia and Niger No. 1, 1 centime black on lilac blue,
Navigation and Commerce, typographed.

Somaliland Protectorate No. 1, ½ anna light green, Queen
Victoria, typographed.

Spanish Morocco No. 1, ¼ centimo blue green, Arms, typographed.

1904

Canal Zone No. 1, 2 cents rose, Map of Panama, engraved.

1905

Rio de Oro No. 1, 1 centimo blue green, King Alfonso XIII,
typographed.

1906

Brunei No. 1, 1 cent violet and black, Crown, engraved.

Maldive Islands No. 1, 2 cents orange brown, King Edward
VII, typographed.

Martinique No. 1, 5c on 20c red on green, Commerce,
typographed.

Mohéli No. 1, 1 centime black on lilac blue, Navigation
and Commerce, typographed.

Upper Senegal and Niger No. 1, 1 centime slate, Gen. Louis
Faidherbe, typographed.

1907

British Solomon Islands No. 1, ½ penny ultramarine, War
Canoe, lithographed.

Middle Congo No. 1, 1 centime olive gray and brown,
Leopard, typographed.

1908

New Hebrides (Br.) No. 2, 2 pence violet and orange,
King Edward VII, typographed.

New Hebrides (Fr.) No. 1, 5 centimes green, Kagu, typographed.

Nyasaland Protectorate No. 1, 1 shilling green, King Edward VII, typographed.

1910

Malaya—Trengganu No. 1, 1 cent gray green, Sultan Zena-
labidin, typographed.

1911

Gilbert and Ellice Islands No. 1, ½ penny green, King
Edward VII, typographed.

Malaya—Kelantan No. 1, 1 cent gray green, Governmental
Symbols, typographed.

1912

Italy—Aegean Islands No. 1, 25 centesimi blue, King Victor Emmanuel III, typographed.

Libia No. 1, 1 centesimo brown, King Victor Emmanuel III, typographed.

Liechtenstein No. 1, 5 heller yellow green, Prince Johann II, typographed.

Malaya—Kedah No. 1, 1 cent green and black, Sheaf of Rice, engraved.

Tibet No. 1, ⅙ trangka green, Lion, typographed, imperforate.

1913

Albania No. 1, 2½ piasters violet brown, Albanian Double Eagle, typographed.

Australia No. 1, ½ penny yellow green, Kangaroo and Map, typographed.

Quelimane No. 1, ¼ centavo on ½ avo blue green, Vasco da Gama, typographed.

South Africa No. 1, 2½ pence deep blue, George V, engraved.

Tete No. 1, ¼ centavo on ½ avo blue green, Vasco da Gama, typographed.

Thrace No. 1, 10 lepta on 20 paras rose, Tughra, typographed.

Trinidad and Tobago No. 1, ½ penny green, Britannia, typographed.

1914

Epirus No. 1, 1 lepton black and blue, Seal, handstamped, imperforate.

New Britain No. 1, 1 penny brown, Kaiser's Yacht, typographed.

Nigeria No. 1, ½ penny green, King George V, typographed.

1915

Bushire No. 1, 1 chahi green and orange, Shah Ahmed, typographed and engraved.

North West Pacific Islands No. 1, 2 pence gray, Kangaroo and Map, typographed.

Ubangi No. 1, 1 centime olive gray and brown, Leopard, typographed.

1916

Cape Juby No. 1, 5 centimos rose, King Alfonso XIII, typographed.

Hejaz No. 1, ¼ piaster green, Carved Design, typographed.

Ile Rouad No. 1, 5 centimes green, Liberty, Equality and Fraternity, typographed.

Kionga No. 1, ½ centavo on 100 reis blue on blue, King Carlos, typographed.

Nauru No. 1, ½ penny green, King George V, typographed.

1917

Mesopotamia No. N1, ¼ anna on 20 paras red lilac, Obelisk of Theodosius, lithographed.

1918

Czechoslovakia No. 1, 3 haleru red violet, Hradcany at Prague, typographed, imperforate.

Estonia No. 1, 5 kopecks pale red, "Eesti Post," lithographed, imperforate.

Fiume No. 1, 10 filler rose, Harvesting, typographed.

Jugoslavia No. 1L1, 3 heller olive green, View of Deboj, engraved.

Latvia No. 1, 5 kapeikas carmine, Arms, lithographed, imperforate.

Lithuania No. 1, 10 skatiku black, Numeral and Name, typeset.

Palestine No. 1, 1 piaster deep blue, "E.E.F." and Numerals, lithographed, rouletted.

South Russia No. 1, 25 kopecks on 1k dull orange yellow, Arms, typographed.

Ukraine No. 1, 3½ rubles black and gray, Arms, typographed.

Western Ukraine No. 1, 5 shagiv on 15 heller dull red, Emperor Karl I, typographed.

1919

Armenia No. 1, 60 kopecks on 1k orange, Arms, typographed.

Azerbaijan No. 1, 10 kopecks green, blue, red and black, Standard Bearer, lithographed, imperforate.

Batum No. 1, 5 kopecks green, Tree, lithographed, imperforate.

Cilicia No. 2, 2 paras red lilac, Obelisk of Theodosius, lithographed.

Georgia No. 12, 10 kopecks blue, St. George, lithographed, perforate or imperforate.

Siberia No. 1, 35 kopecks on 2k dull green, Arms, typographed.

Syria No. 1, 1 millieme gray, Liberty, Equality and Fraternity, typographed.

1920

Aguera, La, No. 1, 1 centimo blue green, King Alfonso XIII, typographed.

Allenstein No. 1, 5 pfennigs green, Germania, typographed.

Castellorizo No. 1, 1 centime gray, Liberty, Equality and Fraternity, typographed.

Central Lithuania No. 1, 25 fennigi red, Coat of Arms, typographed, perforate or imperforate.

Danzig No. 1, 5 pfennigs green, Germania, typographed.

Eastern Silesia No. 1, 1 heller dark brown, Hradcany at Prague, typographed, imperforate.

Far Eastern Republic No. 2, 2 kopecks green, Coat of Arms, typographed.

Marienwerder No. 1, 5 pfennigs green, Allegory of Allied Plebiscite Supervision, lithographed.

Memel No. 1, 5 pfennigs green, Germania, typographed.

North Ingermanland No. 1, 5 pennia green, Arms, lithographed.

Saar No. 1, 2 pfennigs gray, Germania, typographed.

Schleswig No. 1, 2½ pfennigs gray, Arms, typographed.

Trans-Jordan No. 1, 1 millieme dark brown, "E.E.F." and Numerals, typographed.

Upper Silesia No. 1, 2½ pfennigs slate, Numeral, typographed.

Upper Volta No. 1, 1 centime brown violet and violet, Camel and Rider, typographed.

Wallis and Futuna Islands No. 1, 1 centime green, Kagu, typographed.

1921

Dalmatia No. 1, 5 centesimi on 5c green, King Victor Emmanuel III, typographed.

East Africa and Uganda Protectorates (Kenya, Uganda and Tanganyika) No. 1, 1 cent black, King George V, typographed.

Niger No. 1, 1 centime brown violet and violet, Camel and Rider, typographed.

Tanganyika No. 1, 12 cents gray, King George V, typographed.

1922

Ascension No. 1, ½ penny green and black, Government House, typographed.

Barbuda No. 1, ½ penny green, King George V, typographed.

Chad No. 1, 1 centime red and violet, Leopard, typographed.

Ireland No. 1, ½ penny green, King George V, typographed.

Karelia No. 1, 5 pennia dark gray, Bear, lithographed.

1923

Corfu No. 1, 5 centesimi green, King Victor Emmanuel III, typographed.

Cyrenaica No. 1, 20 centesimi olive green and brown orange, Jesus Preaching, typographed.

Iraq No. 1, ½ anna olive green, Sunni Mosque, engraved.

Kuwait No. 1, ½ anna green, King George V, typographed.

Saseno No. 1, 10 centesimi claret, King Victor Emmanuel III, typographed.

South-West Africa No. 1, ½ penny green, King George V, typographed.

Tripolitania No. 1, 20 centesimi olive green and brown orange, Jesus Preaching, typographed.

1924

Algeria No. 1, 1 centime dark gray, Liberty, Equality and Fraternity, typographed.

Lebanon No. 1, 10 centimes on 2c violet brown, Liberty, Equality and Fraternity, typographed.

Mongolia No. 1, 1 cent gray brown, Scepter of Indra, lithographed.

Ruanda-Urundi No. 6, 5 centimes orange yellow, Ubangi Woman, engraved.

Southern Rhodesia No. 1, ½ penny dark green, King George V, engraved.

Spanish Sahara No. 1, 5 centimos blue green, Moor and Camel, typographed.

1925

Alaouites No. 1, 10 centimes on 2c violet brown, Liberty, Equality and Fraternity, typographed.

Nejd (Saudi Arabia) No. 1, 5 paras ocher, Istanbul General Post Office, typographed.

New Guinea No. 1, ½ penny orange, Native Huts, engraved.

Northern Rhodesia No. 1, ½ penny dark green, King George VI, engraved.

Oltre Giuba No. 1, 1 centesimi brown, Arms, typographed.

1926

Tannu Tuva No. 1, 1 kopeck red, Wheel of Life, typographed.

Yemen No. 1, 2½ bogaches black, Crossed Daggers, typographed, imperforate.

1928

Andorra (Sp.) No. 1, 2 centimos olive green, King Alfonso XIII, engraved.

1929

Vatican City No. 1, 5 centesimi dark brown, Papal Arms, engraved.

1931

Andorra (Fr.) No. 1, 1 centime gray, Liberty, Equality and Fraternity, lithographed.

Latakia No. 1, 10 centimes red violet, View of Hama, lithographed.

1932

Inini No. 1, 1 centime gray lilac and greenish blue, Carib Archer, typographed.

Italian Colonies No. 1, 10 centesimi gray black, Giovanni Boccaccio, photogravure.

Manchukuo No. 1, ½ fen gray brown, Pagoda, lithographed.

1933

Bahrain No. 1, 3 pies gray, King George V, typographed.

Basutoland No. 1, ½ pence emerald, King George V, engraved.

1936

French Equatorial Africa No. 1, 1 centime brown violet, Timber Raft, photogravure.

1937

Aden No. 1, ½ anna light green, Dhow, engraved.

Burma No. 1, 3 pies slate, King George V, typographed.

1938

Alexandretta No. 1, 10 centimes violet brown, View of Hama, lithographed, perforate.

Greenland No. 1, 1 öre olive black, King Christian X, engraved.

Italian East Africa No. 1, 2 centesimi orange, Antelope, photogravure.

1939

Czechoslovakia—Bohemia and Moravia No. 1, 5 haleru dark ultramarine, Coat of Arms, engraved.

Czechoslovakia—Carpatho-Ukraine No. 1, 3 koruny ultramarine, View of Jasina, engraved.

Czechoslovakia—Slovakia No. 1, 300 halierov on 10 korune blue, Castle Ruins, engraved.

Hatay No. 1, 10 santims on 20 paras deep orange, Kemal Ataturk, typographed.

1940

Pitcairn Islands No. 1, ½ penny blue green and orange, Orange Cluster and King George VI, engraved.

1941

Croatia No. 1, 50 paras orange, King Peter II, typographed.

Ifni No. 1, 1 centimo green, Numeral and "Estado Español," lithographed, imperforate.

1943

French West Africa No. 1, 1.50 francs dark violet, Diourbel Mosque, typographed.

1944

Muscat and Oman No. 1, 3 pies slate, King George VI, typographed.

1947

Pakistan No. 1, 3 annas slate, King George VI, typographed.

Trieste No. 1, 25 centesimi bright blue green, Torch, photogravure.

1948

Israel No. 1, 3 mils orange, Coin, typographed.

Malaya—Malacca No. 1, 10 cents purple, King George VI and Queen Elizabeth, photogravure.

Malaya—Penang No. 1, 10 cents purple, King George VI and Queen Elizabeth, photogravure.

Malaya—Perlis No. 1, 10 cents purple, King George VI and Queen Elizabeth, photogravure.

Ryukyu Islands No. 1, 5 sen magenta, Cycad, typographed.

Singapore No. 1, 1 cent black, George VI, typographed.

Tokelau Islands No. 1, ½ penny red brown and rose lilac, Map and Scene, engraved.

1949

German Democratic Republic No. 48, 50 pfennigs light blue and dark blue, Pigeon, Letter and Globe, lithographed.

Spanish West Africa No. 1, 4 pesos dark gray green, Native, lithographed.

1950

Dutch New Guinea No. 1, 1 cent slate blue, Numeral, photogravure.

Indonesia No. 333, 15 sen red, Mountain, Palms and Flag, photogravure.

1951

Cambodia No. 1, 10 centimes dark blue green, Apsaras, engraved.

Laos No. 1, 10 cents dark green and emerald, Boat on Mekong River, engraved.

United Nations No. 1, 1 cent magenta, Peoples of the World, engraved.

Viet Nam No. 1, 10 cents olive green, Bongour Falls, photogravure.

1952

Tristan da Cunha No. 1, ½ penny purple, King George VI and Colony Badge, engraved.

1956

Morocco No. 1, 5 francs bright blue and indigo, Sultan Mohammed V, engraved.

1957

Ghana No. 1, 2 pence rose red, Kwame Nkrumah, photogravure.

Qatar No. 1, 1 naye paise light brown, Queen Elizabeth II, photogravure.

1958

Christmas Island No. 1, 2 cents yellow orange, Queen Elizabeth II, engraved and typographed.

United Arab Republic No. 1, 10 milliemes yellow and green, Maps of Egypt and Syria, photogravure.

1959

Central African Republic No. 1, 15 francs blue, carmine, green and yellow, Premier Barthelemy Boganda and Flag, engraved.

Mali No. 1, 25 francs green, carmine and deep claret, Flag and Map, engraved.

1960

Rio Muni No. 1, 25 centimos dull violet blue, Boy and Missionary, photogravure.

1961

Trucial States No. 1, 5 naye paise emerald, Palm Trees, photogravure.

1962

Bhutan No. 1, 2 chetrum red and gray, Postal Runner, lithographed.

Burundi No. 1, 25 centimes dark green and dull orange, Littonia, photogravure.

Rwanda No. 1, 10 centimes brown and gray green, Gregoire Kayibanda and Map of Africa, photogravure.

West New Guinea No. 1, 1 cent vermilion and yellow, Queen Juliana, photogravure.

1963

British Antarctic Territory No. 1, ½ penny dark blue, Queen Elizabeth II, engraved.

Cocos Islands No. 1, 3 pence dark red brown, Copra Industry, engraved.

Dubai No. 1, 1 naye paise dull blue and carmine, Hermit Crab and Sultan, lithographed.

Kenya No. 1, 5 cents blue, buff and dark brown, Tree Tops Hotel and Elephants, photogravure.

Malaysia No. 1, 10 sen violet and yellow, Map of Malaya, photogravure.

Sharjah and Dependencies No. 1, 1 naye paise light blue, green and pink, Sheik Saqr bin Sultan al Qasimi, photogravure.

South Arabia No. 1, 15 cents black and red, Red Cross and Queen Elizabeth II, lithographed.

South Georgia No. 1, ½ penny dull red, Queen Elizabeth II and Reindeer, engraved.

1964

Abu Dhabi No. 1, 5 naye paise bright yellow green, Sheik Shakbut bin Sultan, photogravure.

Ajman No. 1, 1 naye paise multicolored, Sheik Rashid bin Humaid, photogravure and lithographed.

Fujeira No. 1, 1 naye paise, multicolored, Sheik Mohammed bin Hamad al Sharji, photogravure and lithographed.

Malawi No. 1, 3 pence dark green and light olive green, Dr. H. Kamuzu Banda and Monument, photogravure.

Ras al Khaima No. 1, 5 naye paise brown and black, Sheik Saqr bin Mohammed al Qasimi, photogravure.

Sabah No. 1, 1 cent light red brown and green, Queen Elizabeth II and Payau, engraved.

Tanganyika and Zanzibar No. 1, 20 cents blue and emerald, Map of Tanganyika and Zanzibar, photogravure.

Umm al Qiwain No. 1, 1 naye paise multicolored, Sheik Ahmad bin Rashid al Moalla, photogravure and lithographed.

Zambia No. 1, 3 pence blue, brown and green, President Kenneth D. Kuanda and Victoria Falls, photogravure.

1966

Botswana No. 1, 2½ cents multicolored, National Assembly Bldg., photogravure.

Guyana No. 1, 1 cent black, Queen Elizabeth II and Georgetown General Post Office, engraved and lithographed.

Lesotho No. 1, 2½ cents brown, black and red, Chiefs Moshoeshoe I and II, photogravure.

Lesotho

CHAPTER 7

Using That Handiest Tool
— the Catalogue

ANYONE *can* collect stamps without a catalogue, but it's like trying to sail across the Atlantic in a sloop without a chart. You can easily lose your way, you can't compete with your fellow hobbyists, and you miss more than half the fun.

If you want to know more about your stamps and the business of collecting them rather than to be a mere accumulator, you must have a catalogue. A good catalogue contains the amassed knowledge gathered by generations of collectors. The pioneer collectors, of course, did not have these detailed lists to guide them and were compelled to compile the lists themselves, which they did with painstaking research. This detailed research also characterizes the work of today's catalogue editors. Although they are more fortunate than their forerunners in having the lists and catalogues of preceding generations on which to base their findings, the work of listing new issues, revising old listings, and entering new varieties still requires a tremendous knowledge of philately and a strict attention to minute details.

Basically a catalogue is a compact, illustrated list of stamps arranged in sets. But it can be much more than that. In addition to giving all philatelic details of the stamps listed, the catalogue provides an insight into the cultural and political aspects of the issuing countries.

The Scott Catalogue, which originated as a monthly price list in 1867, arranges the stamps under country headings, which appear alphabetically in various groups. Each country heading gives the geographical, political and monetary details of the country. The stamps are listed in subheadings in chronological order of issue. First are the regular issues, followed by the semipostal stamps, the airmails, the officials, postage dues, postal-tax stamps, newspaper stamps, etc. Each of these categories has a capital letter preceding the catalogue number to distinguish one group from another. When there is no letter before the number, the stamp is a regular issue. The letter "B" shows that the stamp is a semipostal; "J" means that it is a postage due; "RA" is for postal tax, etc.

Despite the size of the Scott Catalogue, finding a stamp in it is usually simple. First, look at your stamp to learn the name of the issuing country. Over 95 per cent of the world's stamps have the country's name in Roman letters, and it is fairly easy to identify the country. A bit of simple translation may be necessary. The inscription "République du Niger," for instance, would be "Niger Republic." Some of the more confusing inscriptions, particularly those in unfamiliar Greek or Cyrillic alphabets, can be readily found in the "Stamp Identifier" section of this Handbook.

Once you have determined the country, the best way to find the page where it is *listed* in the Catalogue itself is to check the *Index and Identifier* at the back of the Catalogue. Although this may sound like a ridiculously easy step, a surprising number of people do not use the Index and waste time thumbing through the Catalogue trying to find a country.

Now, open the Catalogue to the country con-

wn 1.25 8
e ('12) 1.15 85
3.00 60
own 10.00 50

9 Surcharged:

35
ØRE
FRIMÆRKE

d

Surcharge.
wn. (112) *Perf. 13.*
16ö slate brown 3.00 3.00
Inverted frame 45.00 45.00

14x13½.
n 20ö rose & gray 2.50 2.50
a. Inverted frame 18.50 18.50

k Surcharge.
ö on 32ö green 3.25 3.25

neral Post Office at Copenhagen
A15

d. Two Crowns. (113)
Engraved. *Perf. 13.*
5kr dark red 60.00 15.00
See No. 135.

Wmk. 114

Typographed.
Wmkd. Multiple Crosses. (114)
-30 *Perf. 14x14½.*
A10 1ö deep orange ('14) 15 5
a. Booklet pane of 6, (2 No. 85, 2 No. 91 + 2 labels) 5.00
" 2ö carmine ('13) 30 5
a. Imperf., (pair) 100.00 100.00
b. Booklet pane, 4 + 2 labels 5.00
7 " 3ö gray ('13) 55 6
8 " 4ö blue ('13) 65 5
a. Half used as 2ö on cover 55.00
89 " 5ö dark brown ('21) 25 4
a. Imperf., (pair) 135.00 135.00
b. Booklet pane, 4 + 2 labels 2.00
90 " 5ö light green ('30) 35 4
a. Booklet pane, 4 + 2 labels 2.00
b. Booklet pane of 50
91 " 7ö apple green ('26) 35 6
a. Booklet pane, 4 + 2 labels 5.00
92 " 7ö dark violet ('30) 65 20
93 " 8ö gray ('21) 35 10
94 " 10ö green ('21) 30 4
a. Imperf., (pair) 250.00
b. Booklet pane, 4 + 2 labels 2.00
95 " 10ö bistre brown ('30) 25 3
a. Booklet pane, 4 + 2 labels 2.00
b. Booklet pane of 50 60 18

King Christian X
A16 A17

1913-28
97 A16 5ö green ('13) 20 4
a. Booklet pane of 4
98 " 7ö orange ('18) 35 8
99 " 8ö dark gray ('20) 1.00 50
100 " 10ö red ('13) 25 4
a. Imperf., (pair) 125.00
b. Booklet pane of 4
101 " 12ö gray green ('18) 1.25 1.00
102 " 15ö violet ('13) 40 5
103 " 20ö deep blue ('13) 1.00 5
104 " 20ö brown ('21) 30 4
105 " 20ö red ('26) 30 6
106 " 25ö dark brown ('13) 1.35 8
107 " 25ö brown & black ('20) 2.75 18
108 " 25ö red ('22) 40 5
109 " 25ö yellow green ('25) 45 6
110 " 27ö vermilion & black ('18) 4.25 4.25
111 " 30ö green & black ('18) 1.35 10
112 " 30ö orange ('21) 45 15
113 " 30ö dark blue ('25) 55 10
114 " 35ö orange ('13) 1.65 12
115 " 35ö yellow & black ('19) 60 15
116 " 40ö violet & blk. ('18) 1.25 12
117 " 40ö gray blue & black ('20) 1.35 15
118 " 40ö dark blue ('22) 1.00 20
119 " 40ö orange ('25) 55 8
120 " 50ö claret ('13) 4.50 60
121 " 50ö claret & black ('19) 2.75 8
122 " 50ö light gray ('21) 90 7
123 " 60ö brown & ultra-marine ('19) 1.65 12
124 " 60ö greenish bl. ('21) 1.00 8
125 " 70ö brown & green ('20) 1.65 10
126 " 80ö blue green ('15) 5.00 2.25
127 " 90ö brown & red ('20) 1.35 15
128 " 1kr brown & blue ('22) 7.00 15
129 " 2kr gray & claret ('25) 18.00 2.35
130 " 5kr violet & brown ('27) 4.00 1.85
131 " 10kr vermilion & yellow green ('28) 60.00 7.50

Engraved.
132 A17 1kr yellow brown ('13) 8.50 15
133 " 2kr gray ('13) 12.00 70
134 " 5kr purple ('20) 3.50 55
135 A15 5kr dark red ('15) 65.00 12.00

Nos. 87 and 98, 89 and 94, 89 and 104, 90 and 95, 97 and 103, 100 and 102 exist se-tenant in coils for use in vending machines.

Nos. 46 and O10 Surcharged in Black

DANMARK
80
ØRE
POSTFRIM.

e

1915 *Perf. 13* **Wmkd. Crown. (112)**
136 A6 (*c*) 80ö on 12ö slate & dull lake 9.00 9.00
a. Inverted frame 80.00 80.00
137 O1 (*e*) 80ö on 8ö carmine 9.00 9.00
a. "POSTERIM" 20.00 20.00

Newspaper Stamps Surcharged

POSTFRIM
ØRE 27 ØRE
DANMARK

On Issue of 1907.
1918 *Perf. 13* **Wmkd. Crown. (113)**
138 N1 27ö on 1ö olive 20.00 20.00
139 " 27ö on 5ö blue 20.00 20.00
140 " 27ö on 7ö carmine 20.00 20.00
141 " 27ö on 10ö dp. lilac 20.00 20.00
142 " 27ö on 68ö yellow brown 3.00 3 00
143 " 27ö on 5kr rose & yellow green 1.00 1.00
144 " 27ö on 10kr bistre & blue 1.65 1.65

On Issue of 1914–15.
Wmkd. Multiple Crosses. (114)
Perf. 14x14½.
145 N1 27ö on 1ö olive gray 90 90
146 " 27ö on 5ö blue 1.75 1.75
147 " 27ö on 7ö rose 1.00 1.00
148 " 27ö on 8ö green 1.25 1.25
149 " 27ö on 10ö deep lilac 90 90
150 " 27ö on 20ö green 1.25 1.25
151 " 27ö on 29ö orange yellow 1.00 1.00
152 " 27ö on 38ö orange 10.00 10.00
153 " 27ö on 41ö yellow brown 1.75 1.75
154 " 27ö on 1kr blue grn. & maroon 80 80

1919
No. 97 Surcharged

2
ØRE

155 A16 2ö on 5ö green 60.00 45.00
a. Inverted surch.

This stamp was issued in the Faroe Islands. Excellent counterfeits of this surcharge are known.

Kronborg Castle
A20

Sonderborg Castle
A21

Roskilde Cathedral
A22

Typographed.
1920 ***Perf. 14½x14, 14x14½.***
156 A20 10ö red 70 8
157 A21 20ö indigo 80 7
158 A22 40ö dark brown 1.85 55

This issue was to commemorate the reunion of Northern Schleswig with Denmark.

1921
159 A20 10ö green 70 8
160 A22 40ö dark blue 2.50 60

1921-22
Stamps of 1918 Surcharged in Blue 8 8
161 A16 8ö on 7ö orange ('22) 45 45
162 " 8ö on 12ö gray green 60 60

1921
No. 87 Surcharged 8
163 A10 8ö on 3ö gray 60 60

King Christian X
A23

King Christia
A24

A25

A26

1924 *Perf. 14*
164 A23 10ö green 1
165 A24 10ö green 1
166 A25 10ö green
167 A26 10ö green
168 A23 15ö violet
169 A24 15ö violet
170 A25 15ö violet
171 A26 15ö violet
172 A23 20ö dark brown
173 A24 20ö dark brown
174 A25 20ö dark brown
175 A26 20ö dark brown

Issued to commemorate the 300th the Danish postal service.
The sheets of each value are com of types A23, A24, A25 and A2 groups of four as illustrated.

Stamps of 1921-22 Sur

2

20 20
k

1926
176 A16 (*k*) 20ö on 30ö
177 " (*l*) 20ö on 40ö dark

A27

1926
178 A27 10ö dull g
179 A28 20ö dark
180 " 30ö dark

Issued in commemorati of the introduction of pos

Stamps
Surcharged i

7
m

1926-27
181 A10 (*m*) 7
182 A16 (*n*) 7
183 " (")
184 " (")

Surcharged on
185 O1 (*e*)
186 " (")
187 " (")
188 " (")
189 " (")
190 " (")
191 " (")

cerned and look at your stamp to determine the features of the design. Then look at the pictures of all the stamps under that country until you find the illustration matching your stamp. In countries that issue large numbers of stamps, such as Russia, this can be somewhat time-consuming. Sometimes a year date given on your stamp will help you find it more quickly. The Scott Catalogue features *Indexes of Commemorative Stamps* for the United States and France; these can also be used to locate a particular stamp more easily. Once you have found the matching illustration, note the letter-number given beneath the design. This is called the *type number*. Many beginning collectors often confuse this type number with the italicized catalogue number of the stamp.

Usually, finding the stamp presents little difficulty because a large percentage of the stamps are illustrated. Sometimes, however, it is necessary to note the general characteristics of the design and find a picture with those characteristics. You should then refer to the description of the designs of the other stamps in the set. This description is given in the *design paragraph* which appears in small type directly above the listing of the set. If, for example, the stamp you are looking for is a 10-pence value picturing a church, and the design paragraph reads "10p, St. Matthew's Church," you have probably located the correct stamp. If, however, the design paragraph reads "10p, Lion and lioness," you must continue the search.

Now read the description of the stamp given in the listing, noting the details of denomination, color, perforation, watermark, type of printing and paper. When the stamp is printed in black on colored paper, the color of the paper alone is given in italics

and the black is understood. If no color is given for an overprint or surcharge, it is black. When an overprint or surcharge comes in two or more colors, abbreviations are used in the listing, as (B) or (Bk) Black, (Bl) Blue, (R) Red, (G) Green, etc. When the year, perforation, watermark or printing method are mentioned, the description applies to all succeeding listings until a change is made. If your stamp corresponds to all the details given in the listing, the search is over.

Generally only one stamp will be issued bearing a particular design. In definitive issues, however, the same design may be used for many stamps of different denomination issued at different times. In such instances, the first listing of the stamps will usually have a note at the end of the listing to refer you to other stamps of the same design. If your stamp does not correspond exactly with the stamp in the first listing, you must check each number in the footnote until you find the correct stamp. Differences in watermark, perforation, and color are particularly important here.

The italic number at the left of the type number, the first number in the catalogue column, is the *catalogue number*. This is the number used to refer to a particular stamp. The catalogue numbers may be used as a type of shorthand. When ordering stamps from a dealer, for example, it is not necessary to order "United States #205, type A5b, 5c yellow brown, perf. 12, issued Apr. 10, 1882, used." A simple "U.S. #205, used" is sufficient.

The first price given with a listing is that for an *unused* or mint stamp. The second price at the right is for a *used* or canceled stamp. Prices in italics indicate infrequent sales, lack of pricing information, that the stamp is not known in the condition indicated, or that the market is fluctuating exces-

sively. The absence of price does not necessarily indicate that the stamp is scarce or rare. It may simply mean that the catalogue editors do not have enough information on the market value of the stamp to determine an accurate price. In the United States listings, a dash in the price column means that the stamp is known in a stated form or variety but that information is lacking or insufficient for pricing.

Variations from the so-called normal stamps are listed in smaller type below the regular listings and are designated by lower-case letters of the alphabet. These are called *minor varieties*. When the minor varieties immediately follow the major listing, the catalogue number and type number are understood to be the same.

Now suppose that you have meticulously carried out all of the steps described and still have not found the stamp listed in the Catalogue. What then?

There are several reasons why the stamp may not be in the Catalogue. First, it may have been issued after that edition of the Catalogue went to press. Stamps which were issued too late to be included in the main body of the Catalogue can sometimes be found in the *Addenda* at the back. If the stamp is not in the Addenda, it will be necessary to wait for the next edition or to check the Catalogue supplements which are published monthly.

Perhaps the stamp you are looking for is a speculative or dubious issue that the Catalogue editors are holding under editorial consideration. Or the stamp may be a nonadhesive, cut from an envelope, airletter sheet or wrapper. Postal stationery is a tremendous field in itself, and nonadhesives falling into this category can be found listed in the highly specialized postal stationery catalogues. Or perhaps your stamp is a foreign private local stamp or a foreign revenue. These are not usually listed in

general catalogues but can be found in specialized ones.

If your stamp is none of these, it may be a bogus or phantom stamp masquerading as a postage stamp, but having no postal validity. Or it may be no more than a stamp-size label, privately printed for any one of thousands of different purposes. Semi-official and private stamps and stamplike labels that are not cataloguable are numerous and often puzzling to the beginner.

The important point to remember in trying to identify a stamp is to read the Catalogue carefully, paying close attention to all details. If you are unsuccessful, you should never hesitate to ask the advice of other collectors. No one is able to identify every stamp or stamplike label with complete certainty. Even philatelic experts can have identification problems. But by using the Catalogue and consulting other collectors, you can add tremendously to your knowledge of philately.

[Parts of the foregoing chapter are based on *Scott's Guidebook to Stamp Collecting* by L. N. and M. Williams.]

CHAPTER 8

Stamp Identifier

THE PUZZLERS are not always in Urdu or Cyrillic.

A collector who loves and lives with 19th-century British Colonials will certainly know that "G" overprinted on a Cape of Good Hope adhesive means Griqualand West. But he may have no idea that a stamp inscribed *Offentlig Sak* belongs in Norway under "Officials."

And while a specialist in old German states will easily spot a stamp with "H.R.G.Z.L." on it as a product of Schleswig-Holstein, he may not click on *Sobreporte* as a Colombian postage-due inscription.

In a word, even the highly accomplished collector cannot instantly recognize any old stamp. So it is good to have a handy Identifier such as this:

Note: Order of items is alphabetical by markings on stamps

A.B., ovptd. on Russia—Far Eastern Republic
ACCP—Azerbaijan
Açores—Azores
Afghan, Afghanes—Afghanistan
Africa Occidental Española—Spanish West Africa
Africa Orientale Italiana—Italian East Africa
Afrique Equatoriale Française—French Equatorial Africa
Afrique Occidentale Française—French West Africa
Alexandrie—French Offices in Egypt
Algérie—Algeria
Allemagne Duitschland—Belgian Occupation of Germany
A.M.G./F.T.T.—Allied Occupation of Trieste
A.M.G./V.G.—Allied Occupation of Venezia Giulia

Algeria

A.M. Post—Allied Military Government in Germany
Andorre—Andorra (French)

Andorra

Belgium, France, many French colonies (post-age due)

Anna, ovptd. on France—French Offices in Zanzibar
A.O., ovptd. on Congo—Belgian Occupation of German East Africa
A.O.F., ovptd. on France—French West Africa
A.O.I., ovptd. on Italy—Italian East Africa
A payer, Te betalen—Belgium (postage due)
A perçevoir—Belgium, France, many French colonies (post-age due)
A.R.—Colombia, Montenegro, Panama, Chile (acknowledgment of receipt)
Arabie Soudite—Saudi Arabia
Archipel des Comores—Comoro Islands
A receber—Portugal and colonies (postage due)
A & T—Annam & Tonkin
Aunus, ovptd. on Finland—Finnish Occupation of Russia
Avisporto—Denmark (newspaper)

Denmark (newspaper stamp)

B, ovptd. on Straits Settlements—Bangkok
Baghdad, ovptd. on Turkey—Mesopotamia
Baj—Roman States
Bajar Porto—Indonesia (postage due)
Baranya—Serbian Occupation of Hungary
Basel—Switzerland
Bayern—Bavaria
B.C.A., ovptd. on Rhodesia—British Central Africa
B.C.M.—Madagascar
B.C.O.F.—Austria (military)
Belgie, Belgique, Belgien—Belgium

Belgium

Belgisch Congo—Congo
Benadir—Somalia (Italian Somaliland)
B.M.A. Malaya—Straits Settlements
B.N.F. Castellorizo—French Occupation of Castellorizo
Böhmen und Mähren—Bohemia and Moravia (Czechoslovakia)
Bosnien-Herzegovina—Bosnia and Herzegovina
Brasil—Brazil
Braunschweig—Brunswick
British Consular Mail—Madagascar
British Somaliland—Somaliland Protectorate
British South African Company—Rhodesia
БЪЛГАРИЯ—Bulgaria

Cape Verde

Cabo—Nicaragua
Cabo Juby—Cape Juby
Cabo Verde—Cape Verde
Carchi—Calchi (Italy, Aegean Islands)
Castelrosso—Castellorizo
CCCP—Russia
C.Ch., ovptd. on French Colonies—Cochin China
C. de Pesos—Philippines
Cechy a Morava—Bohemia and Moravia (Czechoslovakia)
C.E.F., ovptd. on Cameroon—Cameroons Expeditionary Force
C.E.F., ovptd. on India—China Expeditonary Force
Centesimi di corona, ovptd. on Italy—Italian Occupation of Austria
Cesko-Slovenska—Czechoslovakia
CFA, ovptd. on France—Réunion
C.G.H.S., ovptd. on Germany or Prussia—Upper Silesia
Chemins de fer Spoorwegen—Belgium
Chiffre Taxe—France, French Colonies
中華民國郵票—China
Chine, ovptd. on France—French Offices in China
C.I.H.S.—Upper Silesia
C.M.T., ovptd. on Austria—Western Ukraine
Co.Ci., ovptd. on Jugoslavia—Italian Occupation of Jugoslavia
Colonies Postes—French Colonies
Comunicaciones—Spain
Confed. Granadina—Colombia
Confederatio Helvetia—Switzerland
Corean, Coree—Korea
Corona, ovptd. on Italy—Italian Occupation of Austria
Correio—Portugal
Correios e Telégrafos—Portugal

Réunion

China

Ivory Coast

Correos—Cuba, Peru, Spain, Philippines, Dominican Republic
Correos Nacionales—Colombia
Correos y Telegs—Spain
Correspondencia Urgente—Spain
Cos—Coo (Italy, Aegean Islands)
Costa Atlántica B—Zelaya (Nicaragua)
Côte d'Ivoire—Ivory Coast
Côte Française des Somalis—Somali Coast
СРБИЈА —Serbia....
Ct., Ctot., Ctotinki—Bulgaria
Curaçao—Netherlands Antilles
C.X.C.—Jugoslavia

French West Africa

Germany

ДВР , ovptd. on Russia—Far Eastern Republic
Dakar-Abidjan—French West Africa
Danmark—Denmark
Dansk-Vestindiske—Danish West Indies
D.B.L., ovptd. on Russia—Far Eastern Republic
D.D.R.—German Democratic Republic
Deficit—Peru (postage due)
Del Golfo de Guinea—Spanish Guinea
Den Waisen, ovptd. on Italy—Italian Occupation of Jugoslavia
Deutsche Bundespost—Germany
Deutsche Demokratische Republik—German Democratic Republic
Deutsche Neu Guinea—New Britain
Deutsche Ostafrika—German East Africa
Deutschösterreich—Austria
Deutsche Post Osten—German Occupation of Poland
Deutsches Reich—Germany
Deutsch-Sudwestafrika—German South-West Africa
Dienstmarke—Germany, Bavaria, Danzig, Prussia, Saar
Dienst Sache—Württemberg (official)
Diligencia—Uruguay
DJ, ovptd. on Obock—Somali Coast
Djibouti—Somali Coast
Doplata—Poland or Central Lithuania (postage due)
Drzava S.H.S.—Jugoslavia
Due Grana—Two Sicilies

EΔ, ovptd. on Greece—Greek Occupation of Chios
E.A.F., ovptd. on Great Britain—East Africa Forces (Great Britain)

East India Company—India
E.E.F.—Palestine
Eesti—Estonia
EE. UU. de C.—Tolima (Colombia)
Egeo, ovptd. on Italy—Aegean Islands (Italy)
Egypte—Egypt
Einzuziehen—Danzig (postage due)
Eire—Ireland
Ejército Renovador—Sinaloa (Mexico)
El Parlamento a Cervantes—Spain (official)
El Salvador—Salvador
Elua Keneta—Hawaii
Elsas—German Occupation of France
Empire Franc—France
Emp. Ottoman—Turkey
ENAPIΘMON—Greece (postage due)
EΘNIKH—Greece (postal tax)
Escuelas—Venezuela
España—Spain
Estado da India—Portuguese India
Estado Español—Spain
Est Africain Allemand Occupation Belge—Belgian Occupation of
    German East Africa
Estensi, Poste—Modena
Estero, ovptd. on Italy—Italian Offices Abroad
Etablissements Français dans l'Inde—French India
Etablissements de l'Océanie—French Polynesia
Etat Français—France
Etat Ind. du Congo—Congo
Etiopia—Ethiopia, Italian Occupation
Ets. Francs de l'Océanie—French Polynesia
Eupen, ovptd. on Belgium—Belgian Occupation of Germany
EΛΛAC —Greece
EΛΛAΣ—Greece

Fdo. Poo—Fernando Po
Feldpost—Austria, Germany (military)
Fen or Fn.—Manchukuo
Fezzan—French Occupation of Libia
Fiera Campionaria Tripoli—Libia
Filipas, Filipinas—Philippines
Filler—Hungary
Flugpost—Austria, Danzig, Germany (air mail)
Forces Françaises Libres, Levant—Free French Administration
    of Syria

Estonia

Spain

French India

Greece

France

Française—France
Franco—Philippines, Spain
Franco Bollo—Italy, Roman States, Sardinia, Two Sicilies
Francobollo Toscano—Tuscany
Franco Marke—Bremen
Freimarke—Thurn and Taxis (Germany), Prussia, Württemberg, Baden
Frimarke—Denmark, Norway, Sweden

G or GW, ovptd. on Cape of Good Hope—Griqualand West
GAB, ovptd. on French Colonies—Gabon
G & D, ovptd. on French Colonies—Guadeloupe
G.E.A., ovptd. on East Africa and Uganda—German East Africa
General Gouvernement—German Occupation of Poland
Genève—Switzerland
Georgie, Georgienne—Georgia
Gerusalemme—Italian Offices in Turkey
Ghadames—French Occupation of Libia
Giornali Stampe—Italy, Sardinia
Golfo de Guinea—Spanish Guinea
Governo Militare Alleato—Allied Occupation of Italy
GPE, ovptd. on French Colonies—Guadeloupe
Grana—Two Sicilies
Grand Liban—Lebanon
G.R.I., ovptd. on German New Guinea or Marshall Islands—New Britain
Gronland—Greenland
Guiné—Portuguese Guinea
Guinea Española—Spanish Guinea
Guinée—Guinea
Guinée Française—French Guinea
Gültig 9. Armee, ovptd. on Germany—German Occupation of Romania
Guyane—French Guiana
Guy. Franç., ovptd. on France—French Guiana

Greenland

Switzerland

Haute Silésie—Upper Silesia
Haute Volta—Upper Volta
Haute Sénégal-Niger—Upper Senegal and Niger
H.B.A., ovptd. on Russia—Siberia
3.y. H.P., ovptd. on Austria—Western Ukraine
Helvetia—Switzerland
Hirlapjegy—Hungary (newspaper stamp)
ΗΠΕΙΡΟΣ—Epirus
Hrvatska—Croatia, Jugoslavia

Hungary
(newspaper
stamp)

H. I. & U. S.—Hawaii
HOBy—Montenegro
Hoi Hao, ovptd. on Indo-China—French Offices in China
Holkar State—Indore (Indian State)
H.R.Z.G.L.—Schleswig-Holstein

ICC, ovptd. on India—International Control Commission
I.E.F., ovptd. on India—Indian Expeditionary Force
I.E.F. 'D,' ovptd. on Turkey—Mesopotamia
Ile Rouad—Rouad
Imperio Colonial Portugues—Portuguese Africa
Impuesto de Guerra—Spain (war tax)
Inde, Indie—French India
Indo Chine—Indochina
India Portugueza—Portuguese India
Inkeri—North Ingermanland
Instruçao, ovptd. on Portuguese India—Timor
Instrucción—Venezuela
Ionikon—Ionian Islands
Iran, Iraniennes—Persia
Irian Barat—West New Guinea (West Irian)
Island—Iceland
Isole Italiane dell' Egeo, ovptd. on Italy—Aegean Islands (Italy)
Isole Jonie, ovptd. on Italy—Ionian Islands
Istra—Jugoslavia
Itaca, ovptd. on Greece—Ionian Islands
Itä-Karjala—Finnish Occupation of Karelia
Italia, Italiane—Italy

Venezuela

West
New Guinea
(West Irian)

Iceland

日本郵便 —Japan
Jeend, Jhind—Jind (Indian state)
Jugoslavija—Jugoslavia
ЈУГОСЛАВИЈА —Jugoslavia

Japan

Jugoslavia

Finland (military)

Korea

K (with no country name)—Bosnia and Herzegovina
Kamerun—Cameroun
Kaiserliche Königliche Osterreichische Post—Austria
Kalayaan Nang Pilipinas—Japanese Occupation of the Philippines
Karjala—Karelia
Kenttäpostia—Finland (military)
K.G.G.A., ovptd. on Jugoslavia—Carinthia
Kgl. Post. Frm.—Danish West Indies, Denmark
K.K. Post Stempel—Austria, Lombardy-Venetia
K (numeral) K, ovptd. on Russia—Far Eastern Republic
K 60 K, ovptd. on Russia—Armenia
Klaipéda—Memel
대한민국우표—Korea
Korca, Korçë—Albania
Kouang-Tchéou, Kouang-Tcheouwan, ovptd. on Indo-China—Kwangchowan, French Offices in China
KPHTH—Crete
Kraljevina, Kraljevstvo—Jugoslavia
K.U.K.—Austria, Bosnia and Herzegovina
K. Württ.—Württemberg

Lebanon

La Canea, ovptd. on Italy—Italian Offices in Crete
La Georgie—Georgia
Laibach—German Occupation of Jugoslavia
Land-Post Porto-Marke—Baden
Landstormen—Sweden
Lattaquie, ovptd. on Syria—Latakia
Latvija, Latwija—Latvia
Lei, ovptd. on Austria—Austrian Occupation of Romania
Levant—French, British or Polish Offices in Turkey
Liban, Libanaise—Lebanon
Libau, ovptd. on Germany—Latvia
Libya—Libia
Lietuva, Lietvos—Lithuania
Lignes Aerienne F.A.F.L.—Free French Administration of Syria
Lima, ovptd. on Peru—Chilean Occupation of Peru
Lire, ovptd. on Austria—Austrian Occupation of Italy
Lire di Corona, ovptd. on Italy—Dalmatia
Lisso, ovptd. on Italy—Aegean Islands
Litwa Srodkowa—Central Lithuania
Ljubljanska—German Occupation of Jugoslavia
L. Marques, ovptd. on Mozambique—Lourenço Marques

Lokalbref—Sweden (city postage stamps)
Lösen—Sweden (postage due)
Lothringen—German Occupation of France (Lorraine)
LTSR, ovptd. on Lithuania—Russian Occupation of Lithuania
Lubiana—Italian Occupation of Jugoslavia
Luftfeldpost—Germany (military air mail)

Macau, Macav—Macao
Madrid—Spain
Mafeking, ovptd. on Bechuanaland—Cape of Good Hope
Magyar, Magyarorszag—Hungary
Malgache, Malagasy—Madagascar
MAPKA—Finland, Russia, Serbia
Malmédy, ovptd. on Belgium—Belgian Occupation of Germany
Manizales—Antioquia (Colombia)
Marca da Bollo—Italy (revenue)

Italy (revenue)

Marianas Españolas, ovptd. on Phillippines—Mariana Islands
Marianen—Mariana Islands
Maroc—French Morocco, Morocco
Marocco, Marokko—German Occupation of Morocco
Marruecos—Spanish Morocco, Morocco (Northern Zone)
Marshall-Inseln—Marshall Islands
Mauritanie—Mauritania
Mbledhja—Albania
M.E.F., ovptd. on Great Britain—Middle East Forces
Mecklenb. Schwerin—Mecklenburg Schwerin
Mecklenb. Strelitz—Mecklenburg Strelitz
Méjico—Mexico
Memelgebiet—Memel
Menge—Mongolia
Militar Post Portomarke—Bosnia and Herzegovina (postage due)

Morocco

Mill., Milliemes, ovptd. on France—French Offices in Egypt
MN—Korea
Moçambique—Mozambique
Modones—Modena
Mongtze, Mong-Tseu, ovptd. on Indo-China—French Offices in China
Montevideo—Uruguay
Moquea.—Moquegua (Peru)
Mora—Ukraine
Morocco Agencies—British Offices in Morocco
Moyen Congo—Middle Congo
MQE, ovptd. on French Colonies—Martinique
M.V.i.R., ovptd. on Germany—German Occupation of Romania

Mozambique

Netherlands

Finland

New Caledonia

Nandgam—Nandgaon (Indian State)
ПАРА —Serbia
Napoletana—Two Sicilies (Naples)
Nationaler Verwaltungsausschuss, ovptd. on Jugoslavia—German Occupation of Montenegro
N.C.E., ovptd. on French Colonies—New Caledonia
ЛЕВА, ЛЕВЬ —Bulgaria
Ned. Antillen—Netherlands Antilles
Ned. Indie, Nederlandsch-Indie—Dutch Indies
Nederland—Netherlands
Nederlands Nieuw-Guinea—Dutch New Guinea
ПЕН. РЕН. —Finland
Nezavisna Drzava Hrvatska—Croatia
N.F., ovptd. on Nyasaland Protectorate—British Occupation of German East Africa
Nieuwe Republiek—New Republic
Nippon—Japan
Nlle. Calédonie—New Caledonia
ПОРТО МАРКА—Serbia (postage due)
Norddeutscher Postbezirk—Germany (North German Confederation)
Norge, Noreg—Norway
Nouvelle Calédonie—New Caledonia
Nouvelle Hébrides—New Hebrides (French Administration)
ПОЩТА—Serbia
ПОЧТА—Russia
Nr.21, Nr.16—Germany (local officials)
N S B, ovptd. on French Colonies—Nossi-Bé
N. Sembilan—Malaya, Negri Sembilan
N.S.W.—New South Wales
Nueva Granada—Colombia
N.W. Pacific Islands—North West Pacific Islands
N. Z.—New Zealand

Occupation Azirbayedjan, ovptd. on Russia—Azerbaijan
Océanie—French Polynesia
Osterr. Post—Austria
Offentlig Sak—Norway (official)
Oil Rivers—Niger Coast Protectorate
OKCA—Russia, Army of the North
Onza—Spain (official)
Oranje Vrij Staat—Orange River Colony
Orts-Post—Switzerland
O. S.—Norway (official)

Austria

Osten—German Occupation of Poland
Osterreich—Austria
Ostland, ovptd. on Germany—German Occupation of Russia
Oubangui-Chari-Tchad—Ubangi (Ubangi-Shari)

P, ovptd. on Straits Settlements—Malaya, Perak
Pacchi Postali—Italy, San Marino (parcel post)
Packhoi, ovptd. on Indo-China—French Offices in China
Pagó—Cauca, Colombia
Para, Paras—Austrian, German, British, Romanian, Russian,
      French, or Italian Offices in Turkey
Parmensi—Parma
P.C.Ф.C.P.—Russia
PD, ovptd. on French Colonies—St. Pierre & Miquelon
Pechino, ovptd. on Italy—Italian Offices in China
Persanes—Persia
Persekutuan Tanah Melayu—Malaya
Peruana—Peru
Pf—German Offices in China
Pfg.—Estonia under German Occupation
P.G.S.—Malay, Perak (official)
Piastra, ovptd. on Italy—Italian Offices in Crete
Piastre—Italian, British, Russian or French Offices in Turkey
Pilipinas—Philippines
Piscopi, ovptd. on Italy—Italy, Aegean Islands
Plebiscit Slesvig—Schleswig
Plébiscite Olsztyn Allenstein, ovptd. on Germany—Allenstein
РОССIЯ—South Russia
Poczta Polska—Poland
Pohjois Inkeri—North Ingermanland
Polska—Poland
Polynésie Française—French Polynesia
Ponce—Puerto Rico
P. O.—Russian Offices in Turkey
Port Cantonal—Switzerland
Porteado—Portugal and Colonies (postage due)
Porte de Conducción—Peru (parcel post)
Porte de Mar—Mexico
Porte Franco—Peru, Portugal
Port Gdansk, ovptd. on Poland—Polish Offices in Danzig
Portomarke—Bosnia and Herzegovina, Austria (postage due)
Porto Rico—Puerto Rico
Post & Receipt—Hyderabad (Indian State)
Posta 15, Posta 35—Tannu Tuva

Philippines

Great Britain
India,
Kishangarh.

Ireland

German Occupation
of Lithuania

Postage, Postage & Revenue (no country name)—Great Britain, India, Kishangarh
Postage I. E. F. 'D,' ovptd. on Turkey—Mesopotamia
Postas le n'ioc—Ireland (postage due)
Poste aerieo, Poste aerienne (no country name)—Persia
Poste Khedevie Egiziane—Egypt
Poste Locale—Switzerland
Postes Serbes, ovptd. on France—Serbia
Postgebiet Ob. Ost., ovptd. on Germany—German Occupation of Lithuania
Postemarke—Brunswick
Postzegel (no country name)—Netherlands
P. P., ovptd. on France—French Morocco
Preussen—Prussia
Pro Tacna y Arica—Peru (postal tax)
Protectorat Français, ovptd. on France postage due—French Morocco
Pro Tuberculosos Pobres—Spain (postal tax)
Pro Union Iberoamericana—Spain
Provinz Laibach—German Occupation of Jugoslavia
P.S.N.C.—Peru
Pto. Rico—Puerto Rico
РУБ, РУБЛЕЙ—Russia, South Russia, Finland
РУССКАЯ—Russian Occupation of Latvia
рубля, ovptd. on Russia—South Russia

Qarku, Qindar, Qindarka, Qintar—Albania

R, ovptd. on French Colonies—Réunion
Rappen—Switzerland
Rarotonga—Cook Islands
Rayon—Switzerland
Regatul Romaniei, ovptd. on Hungary—Romanian Occupation of Hungary
Regno d'Italia—Italy, Fiume, or Austria under Italian Occupation
Reichspost—Germany
Reis (no country name)—Portugal
Répub. Franc., République Française—France or French Colonies
República Dominicana—Dominican Republic
Rep. di S. Marino—San Marino
República de la N. Granada—Cauca (Colombia)
República Portuguesa Moçambique—Mozambique

República Oriental—Uruguay
República Peruana—Peru
República Portuguesa—Portugal
Republica Sociale Italiana—Italy (Italian Social Republic)
Republika ng Pilipinas—Japanese Occupation of Philippines
République Libanaise—Lebanon
République Rwandaise—Rwanda
Résistance—Free French Administration of Syria
RF—France or French Colonies
R. H.—Haiti
Rheinland-Pfalz—Occupation stamps of Germany
Rialtar Sealadac na Héireann—Ireland
Riau—Indonesia (Riouw Archipelago)
Rigsbank-Skilling—Denmark
RIS, ovptd. on Dutch Indies—Indonesia
RI. Plata F.—Cuba, Philippines
R.O., ovptd. on Turkey—Eastern Roumelia
Rodi—Aegean Islands (Rhodes)
Romagne—Romagna
Romana, Romina—Romania
Roumelie Orientale, ovptd. on Turkey—Eastern Roumelia
Rp—Liechtenstein, Switzerland
R. Colón, ovptd. on Colombia—Panama (registration)
Royaume de l'Arabie Soudite—Saudi Arabia
Royaume du Burundi—Burundi
Royaume du Cambodge—Cambodia
Royaume du Laos—Laos
R.S.M.—San Marino
Ruanda, ovptd. on Congo—German East Africa
Russisch-Polen, ovptd. on Germany—German Occupation of
          Poland
琉球郵便—Ryukyu Islands

Ryukyu Islands

S, ovptd. on Straits Settlements—Malaya, Selangor
Sarre, Saargebiet, Saarland—Saar
Sachsen—Saxony

Spanish Sahara

Sahara España—Spanish Sahara
Salonicco, ovptd. on Italy—Italian Offices in Turkey (Salonika)
S A K—Saudi Arabia
Sandjak d'Alexandrette, ovptd. on Syria—Alexandretta
Saorstát Eireann, ovptd. on Great Britain—Ireland
Sarkari—Soruth (Indian State) (official)
Saurashtra, Sourashtra—Soruth (Indian State)
Scudo—Roman States
Scutari di Albania, ovptd. on Italy—Italian Offices in Turkey (Scutari)
S.d.N. Bureau international du Travail—International Labor Bureau (Switzerland)
Segna Tassa, Segnatasse—Italy (postage due)
Sejm Wilnie—Central Lithuania
Sénégambie et Niger—Senegambia and Niger
Serbien, ovptd. on Bosnia or Jugloslavia—German or Austrian Occupation of Serbia
Sevilla-Barcelona—Spain
Shanghai, ovptd. on U.S.—United States Offices in China
S H Post—Schleswig-Holstein
Shqipenie, Shqiperia, Shqiperise, Shqipni, Shqipnija, Shqyptare—Albania
S. H. S.—Jugoslavia
Siege of Mafeking—Cape of Good Hope
Sirotam, ovptd. on Italy—Italian Occupation of Jugoslavia
Slesvig—Schleswig
Slovensko—Slovakia (Czechoslovakia)
S. Marino—San Marino
Smirne, ovptd. on Italy—Italian Offices in Turkey (Smyrna)
Smyrne, ovptd. on Russia—Russian Offices in Turkey (Smyrna)
S. O., ovptd. on Czechoslovakia or Poland—Eastern Silesia
Sobreporte—Colombia (postage due)
Sociedade de Geographia de Lisboa—Portugal
Société des Nations, ovptd. on Switzerland—Switzerland (official)
Soudan, ovptd. on Egypt—Sudan
Soudan Français—French Sudan
Sowjetische Besatzungs Zone—Russian Occupation of Germany
SPM, ovptd. on French Colonies—St. Pierre & Miquelon
S.Q. Trsta-Vuja—Trieste
Srodkowa Litwa—Central Lithuania
Stadt-Post-Basel—Switzerland
Stati Parm, Stati Parmensi—Parma
S. Tomé e Principe—St. Thomas and Prince Islands

Straordinario—Tuscany (newspaper tax)
S.T. Trsta-Vuja—Trieste
STT-UJA, ovptd. on Jugoslavia—Trieste
S. U., ovptd. on Straits Settlements—Malaya, Sungei Ujong
Suidafrika—South Africa
Suidwes Afrika—South-West Africa
Sultanat d'Anjouan—Anjouan
Suomi—Finland
Suriname—Surinam
Sverige—Sweden
S.W.A.—South West Africa
Syrie, Syrienne—Syria

Sweden

T, ovptd. on Peru—Huacho (Peru)
Tacna y Arica—Peru
ТАКСА—Bulgaria (postage due)
Tanger, ovptd. on French Offices in Morocco—French Morocco
Tanger, ovptd. on Spain—Spanish Morocco (Tangier)
Tangier, ovptd. on Great Britain—British Offices in Morocco
Tassa Gazzette—Modena (newspaper tax)
Taxa de Guerra—Macao, Portuguese Africa, Portuguese Guinea, Portuguese India (war tax)
T.C.E.K.—Turkey (postal tax)
Tchad—Chad
Tchongking, ovptd. on Indo-China—French Offices in China
T. C. Postalari—Turkey
Te Betalen—Netherlands, Netherlands Antilles, Dutch Indies, Surinam, Belgium (postage due)
Telégrafos—Philippines
T.E.O., ovptd. on Turkey, France or French Offices in Turkey—Cilicia, Syria
Terres Australes et Antarctiques Françaises—French Southern and Antarctic Territories
Territoire de l'Inini—Inini
Territoire du Niger—Niger
Territorio de Ifni—Ifni
Territorios Españoles del Golfo de Guinea—Spanish Guinea
Tetuan—Spanish Morocco
Thailand, Thai—Siam

Siam

113

Turkey

West New Guinea

German Occupation of Montenegro

Vatican City

Thrace, ovptd. on Bulgaria—Thrace
Timbre Impérial Journaux—France (newspaper)
Tirane—Albania
Tjeneste Frimaerke—Denmark (official)
Tjenestefrimerke—Norway (official)
Toga—Tonga
To Pay—Great Britain (postage due)
Toscano—Tuscany
Touva, Tuva—Tannu Tuva
Traité de Versailles, ovptd. on Germany—Allenstein
Transjordan—Jordan
TTTT—Dominican Republic (postage due)
T.Ta.C.—Turkey (postal tax air post)
Tumaco—Cauca (Colombia)
Tunis, Tunisie—Tunisia
Türkiye, Turk Postalari—Turkey

ЦАРСТВО—Bulgaria
UG—Uganda
Ukraine, ovptd. on Germany—German Occupation of Russia
Ultramar—Cuba, Puerto Rico, Macao, Portuguese Guinea
UNTEA, ovptd. on Dutch New Guinea—West New Guinea
ЦРНА ГОРА—German Occupation of Montenegro
Urundi, ovptd. on Congo—German East Africa

Vallées d'Andorre—Andorra (French)
Valparaiso Multada—Chile (postage due)
Vancouver—British Columbia and Vancouver Island
Van Diemen's Land—Tasmania
Vaticane—Vatican City
Veneza., Venezolano—Venezuela
Venezia Giulia, Venezia Tridentina, ovptd. on Italy or Austria—
        Italian Occupation of Austria
Vetëkeverria—Albania
Vojenska Posta—Czechoslovakia (Czech Legion in Siberia)
Vojna Uprava—Jugoslavia (Istria)
Vom Empfanger Einzuziehen—Danzig (postage due)
V.R., ovptd. on Transvaal—Cape of Good Hope
VUJA-STT, ovptd. on Jugoslavia—Trieste

Wenden—Russia
West Irian—West New Guinea
Winterhilfe, ovptd. on Italy—German Occupation of Jugoslavia

ХЕЛЕРА —Montenegro

У.С.С.Р.—Ukraine
УСТАВ —Montenegro (postage due)
Yen—Japan
УКРАІНСЬКА—Ukraine
YKp.H.P. ovptd. on Austria—Western Ukraine
Yunnan-Fou, Yunnansen, ovptd. on Indo-China—French Offices in China

Z. Afr. Republiek, Zuid Afrikaansche Republiek—Transvaal
Zalotkop—Poland (Russian Dominion)
Zegelregt—Transvaal
Zeitungs—Austria (newspaper)
Zimska Pomoc, ovptd. on Italy—German Occupation of Jugoslavia
Zona de Ocupatie Romana, ovptd. on Hungary—Romanian Occupation of Hungary
Zona Occupata Fiumano Kupa, ovptd. on Jugoslavia—Italian Occupation of Jugoslavia
Zone Française—French Occupation of Germany
Zuidwest Afrika—South-West Africa
Zurich—Switzerland

CHAPTER 9

Philatelic Literature —
A Selective List

IN EXPLORING a chosen corner of philately the collector who arms himself with knowledge heightens the pleasure of his venture. This knowledge often enables him to spot the rare postmark or the early printing and to avoid the pitfalls of fakery. He knows it pays to listen carefully to the words of those who have traveled the road before him.

Some of the books that carry this knowledge are from small printings and hard to find. Some are in private philatelic libraries that occasionally turn up at auction. Others are still in print and available from dealers in philatelic literature.

Libraries that have some of these studies on their shelves include the Collectors Clubs of New York and Seattle, Boston University Philatelic Library, Enoch Pratt Free Library of Baltimore, Library of Congress, Free Library of Philadelphia, Philatelic Research Society of Oakland, and the public libraries of Chicago, Cleveland, Los Angeles, Milwaukee and Newark (New Jersey).

The following list is drawn from various sources. It incorporates, with permission, much of the List of Philatelic Handbooks prepared by John Freehafer and Helen K. Zirkle and published in the 1956 American Philatelic Congress Book.

AFGHANISTAN

Masson, David P., and Jones, B. G., *The Postage Stamps of Afghanistan*. Madras, 1908.

Meyer, Ferdinand, *La Poste et Les Timbres Poste de L'Afghanistan*. Neuilly, 1881.

Patterson, Frank E., III, *Afghanistan, Its Twentieth Century Postal Issues*. New York, 1965.

ALBANIA

Wallisch, *Albanien und seine Postwertzeichen*.

ALGERIA (*see also* French Colonies and Offices Abroad)

Halden, Ch. ab der, and Beaufond, E. H. de, *Catalogue des Marques Postales et Obliterations de l'Algérie, 1830 à 1876*. Paris, 1949.

ANTIGUA (*see also* British Commonwealth)

Lowe, Robson, *Codrington Correspondence, 1743–1851*. London, 1951.

ARGENTINA

Castro, Esteves Ramón de, *Historia Correos y Telégrafos de la República Argentina*. Buenos Aires, 1934–38.

Deluca, Antonio, *Sellos y Otros Valores Postales y Telegráficos Argentinos*. Buenos Aires, 1939–41.

Kneitschel, Victor, *Catálogo de los Sellos Postales de la República Argentina*. Buenos Aires, 1958.

Peplow, F. J., *The Postage Stamps of Buenos Aires*. London, 1925.

Pont, José Marco del, *Sellos "Rivadavia"—1864–1872*. Buenos Aires, 1946.

Stich, Louis, *Corrientes—the Issues from 1856–1880*. New York, 1957.

ARMENIA

Tchilinghirian, S. D., and Ashford, P. T., *The Postage Stamps of Armenia*. Bristol, England.

ASCENSION (*see also* British Commonwealth)

Leonard, John, *Postage Stamps of Ascension Island*.

AUSTRALIA (*see also* British Commonwealth)

Collas, Phil, *Local Posts of Western Australia*. 1960.

Legge, H. Dormer, *The Kangaroo Issues of Australia*.

Rosenblum, Alec A., *The Stamps of the Commonwealth of Australia*. Melbourne, 1947–48.

Royal Philatelic Society, London, *The Postage Stamps, Envelopes, and Postcards of Australia and the British Colonies of Oceania.* London, 1887.

AUSTRIA

Bundesministerium, *100 Jahre Österreichische Briefmarken.* Vienna, 1950.

Czezik-Müller, *Österreichs Post, Einst und Jetzt.* Vienna, 1929.

Frank, Ph. F. de, *Die Erste Ausgabe von Österreich und Lombardei-Venetien, 1850–1858.* Vienna, 1936.

Gaube, Anton Th., *Die Zeitungsstempelmarken Österreichs und Lombardei-Venetiens.* 1958.

Hurt, Erik F., and Kelly, Denwood N., *The Danube Steam Navigation Company.* Federalsburg, Md., 1950.

Koczynski, *Die Geschichte der Stempelmarken.* 1924.

Kropf, Hans, *Postwertzeichen von Österreich Ungarn.* 1908.

Majetic, Maj. V., *Austrian-Hungarian Catalogue of Field-post Cancels, 1914–1918.*

Mayr-Hanusch, *Handbuch der Stempelmarken Österreich Ungarn.*

Mueller, Edwin, and Mayer, Stephan, *Grosses Handbuch der Abstempelungen von Alt-Österreich und Lombardei-Venetien.* Vienna, 1925.

————, *Zur Typenfrage der Ausgabe 1850.*

Mueller, Edwin, *Die Postmarken von Österreich.* Vienna, 1927.

————, *Handbook of the Pre-Stamp Postmarks of Austria.* New York, 1960.

————, *Handbook of Austria and Lombardy-Venetia Cancellations, 1850 to 1864 Issues.* Vienna.

Sobetzky, Georg, *Austria: Flugpost.* 1929.

BAHAMAS (*see also* British Commonwealth)

Gisburn, Harold G. D., *Postage Stamps and Postal History of the Bahamas.* London, 1950.

BARBADOS (*see also* British Commonwealth)

Bacon, E. D., and Napier, F. H., *The Stamps of Barbados.* 1896.

Bayley, Herbert, *The Post Office in Barbados.* 1933.

Benwell, Basil B., and Britnor, L. E., *The Postal Markings of Barbados.* 1961.

Stephenson, Charles A., *Barbados.* London, 1922.

BASUTOLAND (*see also* British Commonwealth)

Gilbert, G. N., *Historical Notes on Basutoland Postal Matters.*

BELGIAN CONGO

Balasse, Willy, *Catalogue Belgique et Congo Belge* (Tome III, *Congo Belge*). Brussels, 1949.

DuFour, Jean, *Congo—Cinquante ans d'Histoire Postale.* 1962.

Henin, *L'Epopée de l'Air du Congo.* 1961.

BELGIUM

Bertrand, Gustave, *Memorial Philatélique,* Vol. II, *La Belgique.* Montpelier, 1933.

———, *L'Emission de 1869.* 1929.

Grubben, Willy, *Illustrated Catalogue of Essays of Belgium and Congo.* 1933.

Hanciau, L., *La Poste Belge et ses diverses Marques Postales, 1814–1914.* Brussels, 1929.

Herlant, Lucien, *La Poste aux Lettres et Marques Post, 1648–1849.*

———, *La Poste aux Lettres de Liège avant 1849.* 1957.

Smeth, Paul de, *Les Emissions de 1865–1867.* 1932.

BERMUDA (see also British Commonwealth)

Ludington, M. H., *Bermuda "Ship" Type Stamps.* 1955.

———, *Post Offices and Postal Markings of Bermuda.* 1962.

BOLIVIA

Gilbert, *Bolivia 5 Cent Yellow Green of 1861.*

BOSNIA

Glasewald, A. E., *Die Okkupation von Bosnien.*

Oldfield, Herbert R., *Bosnia: Issues of 1879–1900.*

Passer, Adolf, *Postwertzeichen von Bosnien Handbuch.*

BRAZIL

American Philatelic Society, *Imperio do Brazil, 1843–1889.* 1943.

Ayres, Paulo, *Catálogo do Carimbos. São Paulo,* 1937.

Brookman, Lester G., *Brazil: Bull's Eye 100th Anniversary.* New York.

Heinze, Eduard, *Alt Brazilien.* 1919.

Napier, G. S. F., *The Stamps of the First Issue of Brazil.* London, 1923.

BRITISH COMMONWEALTH (*see also* individual countries)

Bond, Nelson S. *Postal Stationery of British North America.*

Britnor, L. E., *Postal History of the British West Indies.*

Easton, John, *British Empire Postage Stamp Design.*

Holmes, L. S., *Handbook and Catalogue of British North America.* Toronto, 1945.

Lowe, Robson, *The Encyclopaedia of British Empire Postage Stamps.* London, 1947.

Potter, W. J. W., *The Printings of King George VI Colonial Stamps.* London, 1952.

Robertson, Alan W., *The Maritime Postal History of the British Isles—Ship Letters.* 1956–1964.

Royal Philatelic Society, London, *The Postage Stamps, Envelopes, Wrappers, Postcards and Telegraph Stamps of the British Colonies, Possessions and Protectorates in Africa.* London, 1895–1906.

————, *The Postage Stamps, Envelopes, Wrappers, Post Cards and Telegraph Stamps of the British Colonies in the West Indies, together with British Honduras and the Colonies in South America.* London, 1891.

Smith, William, *A History of the Post Offices in British North America, 1639–1870.* Cambridge, England, 1920.

BRITISH SOLOMON ISLANDS (*see also* British Commonwealth)

Gisburn, Harold G. D., *British Solomon Islands Protectorate: Its Postage Stamps and Postal History.* Southampton, England, 1956.

BURMA

Smythies, E. A., *Burma: The Japanese Occupation Stamps of 1942–1945.* 1947.

CANADA (*see also* British Commonwealth)

Boggs, Winthrop S., *The Postage Stamps and Postal History of Canada.* Kalamazoo, Mich., 1946.

Deaville, Alfred S., *The Colonial Postal Systems and Postage Stamps of Vancouver Island and British Columbia, 1849–1871.* Victoria, B. C., 1928.

Howes, Clifton A., *Canada: Its Postage Stamps and Postal Stationery.* Boston, 1911.

Jephcott, C. M., Greene, V. G., Young, John H. M., *The Postal History of Nova Scotia and New Brunswick, 1754–1867.* Toronto, 1964.

Konwiser, Harry M., and Campbell, Frank W., *The Canada*

and Newfoundland Stampless Cover Catalog. Verona, N. J., 1946.

Marler, George C., *Canada: Notes on the 1911–1925 Series.* 1949.

Shaw, T. P. G., *The Handbook and Catalogue of Canadian Transportation Postmarks.* Canada, 1963.

Sissons, J. N., *Catalogue of the Revenue Stamps and Telegraph and Telephone Franks of Canada and the Provinces, 1964.* Toronto.

CANAL ZONE

Canal Zone Philatelic Service, *Canal Zone Postage Stamps.* Mount Hope, C. Z., 1961.

CAPE OF GOOD HOPE (*see also* British Commonwealth)

Allis, Gilbert J., *Cape of Good Hope: Its Postal History and Postage Stamps.* London, 1930.

Jurgens, A. A., *The Handstruck Letter Stamps of the Cape of Good Hope from 1792 to 1853 and the Postmarks from 1853–1910.* Capetown, 1943.

Stevenson, D. Alan, *The Triangular Stamps of the Cape of Good Hope.* London, 1950.

CAYMAN ISLANDS (*see also* British Commonwealth)

Aguilar, E. F., and Saunders, P. T., *Cayman Islands, Their Postal History, Postage Stamps and Postmarks.* Great Britain, 1962.

Nicholson, L. C. C., *Jamaican Stamps Used in the Cayman Islands.*

CEYLON (*see also* British Commonwealth)

Crofton, C. S. F., and Jones, B. G., *The Fiscal and Telegraph Stamps of Ceylon.* London, 1911.

Royal Philatelic Society, London, *The Postage Stamps, Envelopes, Wrappers, Post Cards and Telegraph Stamps of British India and Ceylon.* London, 1892.

CHILE

Carreras, *Primeras Emisiones de Chile.*

DeViron, *Chile: Les Premières Emissions, 1853–1866.*

Galvez, Joaquin, *Los Primeros Sellos de Chile.* Chile, 1964.

Palmer, Derek, *Chile: Correos Ingles, Guerra del Pacífico.*

Porter, Harry S., *Chile: Matasellos Usados con las Emisiones sin Dentar.*

Vaca Silva, *Chile: Emissión Provisional Aereo, 1928–1936.*

CHINA

Livingston, L. F., *Classical China*. Baltimore, 1956.

Ma Zung-Sung, *Ma's Illustrated Catalogue of the Stamps of China*. Shanghai, 1948.

Oldfield, Capt. Herbert R., *Stamps of the Treaty Ports of China and Formosa*.

Pappadopulo, S. A., *China and the Treaty Ports*. 1935.

Rosenberg, *Local Posts of China*.

COLOMBIA

Gebauer, Eugenio, *The Air Post Stamps of Colombia*. Caracas, 1963.

Kessler, F. W., *The Air Post Stamps of Colombia*. Brooklyn, N. Y., 1936.

―――, *Departmental Express Stamps*.

Myer, John N., *Studies in the Philately of Colombia*. New York, 1940.

―――, *Tolima's Honda Provisionals*.

COSTA RICA

Bonilla Lara, Alvaro, *Guanacaste Overprints*.

Harland, *Costa Rica: A Minor Plate Study of the Issue of 1862*.

Mechin, R. J., *Costa Rica Issue of 1863*.

Peralta, *Sobrecargas Clásicas de Costa Rica*.

―――, *Sobrecargas de 1911*.

CUBA

Friederich, Rudolf, *Cuba: Y¼ Eine Studie*.

Garcia, Rafael R., *Correo Aereo en Cuba, Primeros Vuelos*. 1937.

Monge, Pedro, *Matasellos Españoles de Ultramar*.

CYPRUS

Castle, Wilfred T. F., *Cyprus, Its Postal History and Postage Stamps*. London, 1952.

CZECHOSLOVAKIA

Bela, Terfi, *Ungarische Vorlaufer Stempel*.

Hirsch, Ervin, and Franek, Jaroslav, *Ceskoslovenske Znamy*. Prague, 1935.

Leitenberger, Friederich, *Handbuch der Tschechosl. Postempel Österr. und Ungar. Herkunt*.

Schultz, *Deutsche Dienstpost in Böhmen-Mähren*.

Velek, John, *The Hradcany Issue*. 1961.

DENMARK

Arnholtz, Svend, *Danske Postempler fra Frimaerketiden.* Copenhagen, 1953.

Gronlund, S., *The Denmark 2 Rigsbank Skilling, 1851–1852.* Copenhagen, 1956.

Hagemann, G. A., *Danmarks og Dansk Vestindiens Frimaerker.* Copenhagen, 1942–51.

Juhl, Mogens, *Denmark: The Engraved Postage Stamps, 1933–1948.* 1948.

————, *Denmark: Postal Booklets.* 1950.

Phillips, Charles J., *Denmark, Catalogue of the 1851–1899 Issues.*

Schmidt-Andersen, J., *The Postage Stamps of Denmark, 1851–1951.* Copenhagen, 1951.

DOMINICAN REPUBLIC

Hennan, Dr. Clarence W., *Dominican Republic, 19th Century Postage Stamps.*

ECUADOR

Haworth, Wilfrid B., *Early Postmarks of Ecuador.*

————, *Notes on the 1c Official of 1896.*

Levi Castillo, Roberto, *Scadta Airmails of Ecuador.* 1960.

Pastor, *Ecuador: Estudio Primera Emissión.*

Salinas, de L., *Ecuador 1928 Overprint Provisionals.*

EGYPT

Blomfield, S., *Postal Markings of Egypt, 1867–1880.*

Boulad, Jean, *Egypt: Les Precurseurs, La Poste Européenne.*

Byam, Dr. William, *Egypt: First Issue of 1866.*

————, *Egypt: Second Issue of 1867.*

Kehr, Ernest A., *The 20th Century Stamps of Egypt.* 1942.

————, *Commemorative Stamps of Egypt.*

————, *The Interpostal Seals of Egypt 1864–1891.*

Lee, George L., *Egypt Royal Imperforate Printings.* 1959.

Mazloum, Ahmed, *Catalogue Zeheri des Timbres-Poste d'Egypte et du Soudan.* 1956.

ESTONIA

Eichenthal, *Illustrated Specialized Catalog.* 1932.

Schultz, *Deutsche Dienspost von 1939–1945.*

Weiner, *Eesti Special. Katalog-Marken, Ganzsachen und Stempel.* 1934.

FALKLAND ISLANDS (*see also* British Commonwealth)

Goodman, F. C. A., *Falkland Islands: Some Facts and Fallacies.* Birmingham, 1927.

Grant, B. S. H., *The Postage Stamps of the Falkland Islands and Dependencies.* London, 1952.

FIJI (*see also* British Commonwealth)

Campbell, *Post Offices and Cancellations of Fiji.* 1958.

Phillips, Charles J., *The Postage Stamps of the Fiji Islands.* London, 1908.

Purves, James R. W., *The Postage Stamps of Fiji, 1878–1902.*

FINLAND

Grosfils-Berger, P., *Les Timbres des Premières Emissions de 1856 à 1889–1895.* Brussels, 1948.

Hellman, E. A., *Die Figurenstempel.*

———, *Eisenbahnmarken Finlands.* 1955.

Kinnunen, *Suomen Laivapostimerkit.* 1930.

Linder, *Finlands Ovalmaerken, 1856–1860.*

Pelander, Carl E., *The Postal Issues of Finland.* 1940.

Posti-Ja Lennatinhallitus Suomen Postilaitoksen Historia, 1638–1938. Helsinki, 1938.

FRANCE

Bertrand, Gustave, *Mémorial Philatélique,* Vol. I., *La France depuis 1880.* Montpelier, 1932.

———, *La France: Premières Emissions de 1849 a 1900,* Vol. IV. Buschwiller, 1948.

Chapier, Georges, *Histoire de la Poste à Lyon.* Lyon, 1965.

Devoitine and Stowsky, *Catalogue des Estampilles et Oblit. Postales de France et Colonies.* 1929.

Dilleman, Paul, *Description Générale des Timbres-Poste de l'Emission de Bordeaux, 1870–1871.* Amiens, 1929.

François, L., *Les Correspondances par Ballon Monté.* 1926.

Frank, P. F. de, *Les Marques Postales de la Grand-Armée par son Histoire, 1805–1808.* Paris, 1949.

Germain, Pierre, *Le 25 Centimes Cérès de 1871 au Type I.* Paris, 1952.

———, *Le 25 Centimes Cérès de 1871 au Type II.* Alençon, 1963.

Jones, Bedford, *History of France, Its Stamps and Cancellations, 1849–1900.*

LePileun, *La Poste par Ballons Montés, 1870–1871.*

Lesgor, Raoul, and Minnegerode, Meade, *The Cancellations on French Stamps of the Classic Issues, 1849–1876.* New York, 1948.

Marconnet, F., *Les Vignettes Postales de la France et de ses Colonies*. Nancy, 1897.

Salles, Raymond, *La Poste Maritime Française*. Paris, 1962.

Vaille, Eugene, *Histoire des Postes jusqu'à la Revolution*.

———, *Histoire Générale des Postes Françaises*. Paris, 1847–1851.

Winnezeele, Baron de, *L'Impression des Timbres Franc par les Rotatives*. 1950.

———, *Les Types des Timbres de France, 1900–1938*.

FRENCH COLONIES AND OFFICES ABROAD (*see also* individual countries)

Stone, Robert G., *French Colonies, the General Issues*. New York, 1961.

Winnezeele, Baron de, *French Colonies and Offices Abroad, A Study of Surcharges*.

FRENCH MOROCCO (*see also* French Colonies and Offices Abroad)

Bonnafous, *Morocco: La Poste Locale*. 1947.

Chapier, Georges, *Les Obliterations du Maroc*. Turnhout, Belgium, 1955.

Exelmans, Comte, and Pomyers, Comte O. de, *Maroc, Postes Françaises*. Amiens, 1948.

Neidorf, Charles, *French Morocco: The 1843–1944 Tour Hassan Issues*. New York, 1953.

GAMBIA (*see also* British Commonwealth)

Dalwick, R. E. R., *Postage Stamps of the Gambia*. Boston, 1953.

Bridge, *The Postmarks of the Gambia*.

Melville, F. J., *The Gambia*.

GABON (*see also* French Colonies and Offices Abroad)

Pomyers, Comte Oliver de, *Les Timbres du Gabon, 1862–1936*.

GERMANY

Busch, Herbert, *Die Unionpost im Besetzten Deutsch Sudwest-Afrika, 1914–1919*. Berlin, 1920.

Friedemann, Albert, *Die Postwertzeichen und Entwertungen der Deutschen Postanstalten in den Schutzgebieten und im Auslande*. Leipzig, 1921.

Kohler, Karl, *Die Briefmarken von Wurttenberg, 1851–1881*. Lorch, 1940.

Lindenberg, Carl, *Die Briefumschlage der Deutschen Staaten*. Leipzig and Berlin, 1892–95.

Mark, Muller, *Alt Deutschland unter der Lupe*.

Ohrt, Paul, *Die Poststempel von Oldenburg*. Chemnitz, 1911.

Piefke, *Geschichte der Bremischen Landespost*. 1947.

Schloss, *Distinguishing Marks of Classic Old German Stamps*. 1948.

Schmidt, K., *Handbuch der Deutschen Privatpostwertzeichen*. Borna-Leipzig, 1939.

Schneider, *Etude-Catalogue des Premiers Timbres de Hambourg*. 1935.

Schupp, Wilhelm, *Die Postwertzeichen des Saargebietes*. Borna-Leipzig, 1935.

Simon, Siegfried, *Handbuch der Baden—Poststempel, Ganzsachen, Postscheine und Marken*. Leipzig, 1936–39.

GREAT BRITAIN

Alcock, R. C., *1841 Penny Red, Archer Plates Die I Pl. 92–101*. Cheltenham, 1950.

Alcock, R. C., and Holland, F. C., *The Postmarks of Great Britain and Ireland*. Cheltenham, 1940.

Alcock, R. C., and Meredith, C. W., *British Postage Stamp Varieties Illustrated*. Cheltenham, 1949.

Bacon, Edward D., *The Line-engraved Stamps of Great Britain*. London, 1920.

Beaumont, K. M., and Adams, H. V., *The Postage Stamps of Great Britain*. Part III. London, 1954.

Bowman, *Great Britain Perfins*. 1959.

Brumell, George, *The Local Posts of London, 1680–1840*. Cheltenham, 1939.

————, *British Post Office Numbers, 1844–1906*. Cheltenham, 1946.

————, *The Franking System in the Post Office, 1652–1840*. 1942.

de Worms, Baron Percy, *Perkins Bacon Records*. London, 1953.

Easton, John, *British Postage Stamp Design*. London, 1943.

Evans, Edward B., *A Description of the Mulready Envelope*. London, 1891.

Ewen, Henry L. E., *A History of Railway Letter Stamps*. London, 1901.

Lillywhite, Bryant, *London Coffee Houses*. London, 1963.

Litchfield, P. C., *Guide Lines to the Penny Black*. London, 1949.

Nissen, Charles, and McGowan, Bertram, *The Plating of the Penny Black Postage Stamps of Great Britain, 1840*. London, 1922.

Osborne, H., *Twopence Blue: Studies of Plates I to XV*. London, 1946.

————, *British Line Engraved Stamps: Repaired Impressions*. London, 1950.

Robertson, Alan W., *A History of Ship Letters of the British Isles*. Pinner, 1955–1962.

Robinson, Howard, *The British Post Office*. Princeton, 1948.

————, *Carrying British Mails Overseas*. New York, 1964.

Seymour, J. B., *The Stamps of Great Britain*. London, 1934.

Staff, Frank, *The Penny Post, 1680–1918*. London, 1964.

Vallancy, F. Hugh, and Oliver, Stanley A. R., *The Postage Stamps of Great Britain, 1840–1922*. London, 1923.

Westley, H. C., *The Postal Cancellations of London, 1840–1890*. London, 1950.

Wilson, John, *The Royal Philatelic Collection*. London, 1952.

GREECE

Hellenic Philatelic Society, *Grèce: Etude sur les Timbres, Grosse Tête de Mercure*. Athens, 1933.

Nicolaides, N. S., *Histoire de la Création du Timbre Grec*, Paris, 1923.

Spink, Ernest W., and Truman, Robert O., *Greece: Large Hermes Heads*. Jamaica, N. Y., 1949.

Zervas, H. G., *Greece* (translated from *Kohl's Handbook*), New York, 1943–44.

GRENADA (*see also* British Commonwealth)

Charlton, Alfred, *The Postal History and Postage Stamps of Grenada*. Leominster, 1955.

GUATEMALA

Freiburghaus, J. G., *Guatemala—1894 Provisionals*.

Lauper, Fred A., *Second Provisional Issue of Guatemala, 1866*. New York, 1952.

Narath, Albert, *Guatemala: Beitraege zur Stempelkunde*. Berlin, 1957.   .

HAITI

Hennan, Dr. C. W., *Haiti, Postal History and Postage Stamps*.

Montes, Leon, *La Timbrologie Haitienne, 1881–1954*. Port-au-Prince, 1954.

Poole, B. W. H., *Haiti, Plating of the First Issue.*

HELIGOLAND
Gadsby, D. J., *Heligoland, Originals and Reprints.*

HEJAZ
Warin, D. F., and Gaskin, J. C., *Postal Issues of Hejaz, Jeddah and Nejd.* London, 1927.

HONDURAS
Green, Irving I., *Honduras: The Black Air Mail.* New York, 1962.

HONG KONG (*see also* British Commonwealth)
Lobdell, H. E., and Hopkins, Adrian E., *Hong Kong and the Treaty Ports.* London, 1949.

Thorndike, E., and Shek, Peter, *The Postage Stamps of Hong Kong.* Hong Kong, 1959.

Webb, F. W., *Hong Kong and the Treaty Ports of China and Japan.* London, 1961.

HUNGARY
Bartha, *Feldpostaemter der Ungarischen Bolschewikiarmee.*

Kropf, Hans, *Die Postwertzeichen des Kaisertums Österreich und der Österreichisch-Ungarischen Monarchie.* Prague, 1908.

Payer, Bela, *Briefmarken des Koenigr. Ungarn.* Berlin, 1920.

ICELAND
Caroe, E. A. G., *Icelandic Posts, 1776–1919.* London, 1948.

Pihl, C. A., *Islands Frimerker—en Kortfattet Oversikt.* Oslo, 1946.

Scherer, Robert W., *Handbook of Icelandic Postal Stationery.* 1957.

Yort, Weiergang, *The "prir" Surcharges of Iceland.*

INDIA
Clarke, Geoffrey, *The Post Office of India and Its Story.* London, 1921.

Cooper, Jal, *Stamps of India.* Bombay, 1951.

———, *Stamps of India Used Abroad.*

Crofton, C. S. F., and Corfield, Wilmot, *The Adhesive Fiscal and Telegraph Stamps of British India.* Calcutta, 1905.

Dawson, L. E., *The Indian Feudatory States.*
——, *One Anna and Two Annas Postage Stamps of India, 1854–1855.* 1949.
Giles, *Handstruck Postage Stamps of India.*
Hausburg, Leslie L. R., *The Postage and Telegraph Stamps of British India.* London, 1907.
Martin, D. R., and Smythies, E. A., *Four Annas of India, 1854–1855.* London, 1930.
Masson, David P., *The Stamps of Jammu and Kashmir.* Lahore, 1901.
Philatelic Society, London, *The Postage Stamps, Envelopes, Wrappers, Post Cards and Telegraph Stamps of British India and Ceylon.* London, 1892.
Sefi, Alexander, and Mortimer, C. H., *The Stamps of Jammu—Kashmir.* London, 1937.
Stewart-Wilson, Charles, and Jones, B. G., *British Indian Adhesive Stamps (Queen's Head) Surcharged for Native States.* Calcutta, 1904.

IRELAND

Alcock, R. C., and Holland, F. C., *The Postmarks of Great Britain and Ireland.* Cheltenham, 1940.
Ewen, Henry L. E., *Irish Railway Stamps.* London, 1906.
Hilliard, *Irish Postage Stamps.*
Ware, P. W., *Postage Stamps of the Irish Free State.* 1924.
Zervas, H. G., *Irish Free State Overprint Issues.*

ISRAEL AND PALESTINE

Heymann, I., and Pertzelan, M., *A Handbook and Catalogue of the Postage Stamps of Israel.* Tel Aviv, 1953.
Hoexter, Dr. W., and Lachman, S., *The Stamps of Palestine.* Haifa, 1959.
Mosden, E., *Israel Catalogue.* New York, 1966.
Pollack, F. W., *Turkish Posts in the Holy Land.* Tel Aviv, 1962.

ITALY AND ITALIAN STATES AND COLONIES

Bertrand, Gustave, *Memorial Philatélique,* Vols. IV and V, *L'Italie.* Amiens, 1934.
Bocchialini, *Parma: Annullamenti 1860–1863, su Franco-bolli Sardo Italiani.*
Bolaffi, Alberto, *The Postmark-Stamps and Postal Cancellations of the Sardinian States, 1851–1863.* New York, 1948.
Caccarelli, *Stato Pontif, 1868, Dentellature di Prova.*

DeMagistis, *Italian States, Italy and Colonies, Marche da Bollo*. 1947.

Diena, Emilio, *I Francobolli del Regno di Napoli*. Milan, 1932.

————, *A History of the Postage Stamps of Sicily*. London, 1925.

————, *The Stamps of the Duchy of Modena*. London, 1906.

————, *Roman States: Counterfeit Stamps Used for Postage*.

Gian, Giorgio dal, *I Timbri Postali ed i "Tagli delle Soldi 4 per lettere" della Republica di Venezia*. Venice, 1950.

Lenars, *Manuel des Timbres des Deux Siciles, Roi Ferdinand*.

Mayer, S., *Napoli: I Francobolli di Transizione del 1861*.

Mezzadri, *Tuscany: Valutazione dei Bolli ed Annullamenti Post*.

Patton, Donald S., *The Romagna*. London, 1953.

Tchilinghirian, S. D., and Bernardelli, R. R., *Stamps of Italy Used Abroad*. London, 1963–1965.

JAMAICA (*see also* British Commonwealth)

Aguilar, E. F., *The Philatelic Handbook of Jamaica*. Kingston, 1949.

Collett, G. W., *Jamaica: Its Postal History, Postage Stamps and Postmarks*. London, 1928.

Johnson, Alfred N., *Jamaica; A Review of the Nation's Postal History and Postage*. Ord, Nebraska, 1964.

Nicholson, L. C. C., *Jamaica Obliterator Marks*. London, 1949.

————, *Jamaica Pre-Stamp Covers*. London.

JAPAN

Boekema, R., and Hedeman, N. F., *Dai Nippon in South East Asia*. The Hague, 1948.

Gely, *Les faux Timbres anciens du Japon et leur expertise, 1871–1875*. 1958.

Ichida, Soichi, *The Dragon Stamps of Japan 1871–1872*. 1959.

————, *The Cherry Blossom Issues of Japan*. 1966.

Peplow, F. J., *Plates of the Stamps of Japan, 1871–1876*. London, 1910.

Woodward, A. M. T., *The Postage Stamps of Japan and Dependencies*. Shanghai, 1928.

JUGOSLAVIA

Haimow, *Jugoslavia Specialized Catalog*. 1928.

Rukavina, *Jugoslavia, Prestamps and Cancels to 1883*.

KOREA

Brady, Lynn R., and Tyler, Varro E., Jr., *Korea: Handbook of Philatelic Forgeries*. Seattle, Wash., 1963.

Dilley, Luther L.L., *Korean Stamp Catalog*. Lusby, Md., 1961.

Kerr, James W., *Korean Kingdom and Empire Philatelic Catalog and Handbook*. Miami, Fla., 1965.

LATVIA

Becker, *Latvia Nos. 1 and 2, Plate Study*.

Meyer-Brehm, Dr. Victor, *Lettland: Beitrag zur Stempelkunde*.

LEEWARD ISLANDS (*see also* British Commonwealth)

Hopkins, A. E., *Postage Stamps of the Leeward Islands*. 1918.

Lloyd, Michael J., *Postage Stamps of the Leeward Islands and Their Cancellations*.

LIBERIA

Beckton, W. D., *Liberia: Plates of the Stamps of 1880*.

Wickersham, C. W., *Liberia: The 1892 Numeral Issue*.

LIECHTENSTEIN

Bertrand, Gustave, *Memorial Philatélique*, Vol. III, *Luxembourg, Switzerland and Liechtenstein*. Montpelier, 1934.

DuVal, Bernard, *Liechtenstein, seine Post und seine Postwertzeichen*. Kayl, 1933.

LUXEMBOURG

Bertrand, Gustave, *Memorial Philatélique*, Vol. III, *Luxembourg, Switzerland and Liechtenstein*. Montpelier, 1934.

Martin, Mathias, *Rundum die Luxembourger Briefmarken*. Luxembourg, 1936.

Mehlem, *Cahiers Luxembourgers*. 1952.

Poss, Nicolas, *Die Post des Herzogtums Luxembourg*. Luxembourg, 1951.

Rhein, Francis, *The Postal History of the Grand Duchy of Luxembourg*, Kalamazoo, Mich., 1941.

Rousseau, Charles, *Evolution of Postal Rates in Luxembourg.* Seattle, 1953.

Wolff, *La Genèse des Deux Premiers Timbres de Luxembourg.*

————, *Les Marques Postales Prephilatéliques.*

MADAGASCAR (*see also* British Commonwealth)

Kricheldorf, *Madagaskar, 1809–1902, Neues Handbuch.* 1959.

MALTA (*see also* British Commonwealth)

Freshwater and Dowling, *Malta Cancellations and Varieties.*

Orme, *Malta ½ Pence Centenary.*

MANCHUKUO

Akagi, Roy H., *The Postage Stamps of Manchoukuo.* New York, 1941.

Pederson, Haag, *Postage Stamps of Manchoukuo.*

Schumann, Alexander, *Manchoukuo Specialized Catalogue.* Shanghai, 1943.

Zirkle, Helen K., *Manchoukuo.* New York, 1965.

MEXICO

Berdanier, Paul F., Jr., *Mexico Airmail Stamps and History of Flights.*

Chapman, S., *The Eagle and Maximilian Stamps of Mexico.* London, 1912.

————, *The Postage Stamps of Mexico from the Commencement in 1856 to the End of the Provisional Period in 1868.* Sevenoaks, 1926.

Odfjell, Abraham, *Stamps of the Postal Districts of Mexico.* Elmhurst, Ill., 1960.

Schatzkes, Joseph, *The Cancellations of Mexico, 1856–1874.*

Smeth, Paul de, and Fayolle, Marquis de, *Les Premières Emissions du Mexique, 1856–1874.* Amiens, 1934.

MONACO

Almasy, Paul G., *Monaco: La Série Charles III, Originals and Forgeries.* 1945.

Chiavassa, *Histoire de Monaco par ses Timbres.*

Delrieu, *Monaco: Marques Postal, 1790–1860.*

MONTENEGRO

Brunel, Georges, *Les Timbres du Montenegro.*

Strandell, Nils, *Montenegro: Tredje Emissiones, 1893–1898.*

Taussig, *Geheimzeichen der Marken Montenegros.*

NEPAL

Haverbeck, Harrison D. S., and Smythies, E. A., *The Postage Stamps of Nepal*. New York, 1952.

NATAL (*see also* British Commonwealth)

Mann, E. W., *Natal—Victorian Postage Stamps*. London, 1940.

NETHERLANDS AND COLONIES

Chase, C., *Histoire et Catalogue des Marques Postales des Dept. conquis sous la Revolution, 1792–1815*.

Hennan, Dr. Clarence W., *Curaçao, 1872–1925*.

Korteweg, P. C., *De Kleinrondstempelis van Netherlands*.

———, *Postdienst en Postempels hier te Lande tot 1811*. 1941.

Nederlandsche Vereeniging van Postzegelverzamelaars, *Handboek der Postwaarden van Nedrl.-Indie*. Haarlem, 1910–24.

Poel, *History and Catalog of Holland Revenues, 1624–1954*.

de Veer, G. W. A., *De Poststukken*. 1947.

NEWFOUNDLAND (*see also* British Commonwealth)

Boggs, Winthrop S., *The Postage Stamps and Postal History of Newfoundland*. Kalamazoo, Mich., 1940.

Dalwick, R. E. R., and Harmer, C. H. C., *Newfoundland Airmails, 1919–1938*. London, 1953.

Konwiser, Harry M., and Campbell, Frank W., *The Canada and Newfoundland Stampless Cover Catalog*. Verona, N. J., 1946.

Wallace, Graham, *The Flight of Alcock and Brown, 14–15 June 1919*. London, 1956.

NEW GUINEA (*see also* British Commonwealth)

Hoffmann, Giesecke G., *New Guinea Catalogue*. 1957.

NEW HEBRIDES (*see also* British Commonwealth)

Jurion, M., *New Hebrides*.

NEW SOUTH WALES (*see also* British Commonwealth)

Houison, Andrew, *History of the Post Office together with an Historical Account of the Issue of Postage Stamps in New South Wales*. Sydney, 1890.

Hull, Arthur F. B., *The Postage Stamps, Envelopes, Wrappers, Postcards and Telegraph Stamps of New South Wales*. London, 1911.

NEW ZEALAND (*see also* British Commonwealth)

Collins, R. J. G., *The 2s Pictorial of 1935–1942*. Christchurch, 1951.

Collins, R. J. G., and Fathers, H. T. M., *The Postage Stamps of New Zealand*. Wellington, 1938–50.

Lee, G. R., *The Penny Universal of New Zealand*. Wellington, 1953.

Robinson, Howard, *A History of the Post Office in New Zealand*. Wellington, 1964.

NORWAY

Anderssen, Justus, and Dethloff, Henrik, *Norges Frimaerker, 1855–1924*. Christiania, 1925.

Goodfellow, B., *Study of Types of 4sk, 1863–1866*.

———, *Study of Types of 1877–1878 and 1894–1909*.

Jellestad, Johannes, and Odfjell, Abraham, *Norway: Plating of the 1st Issues*. Jamaica, N. Y., 1948.

Sannes, Stian, *The Stamps of the Private Byposts*. 1944.

ORANGE FREE STATE

Fenn, A. Cecil, *Orange Free State Postal Markings, 1868–1910*.

Geldhof, A. E., *Stamps of the Orange Free State*. Federalsburg, Md., 1938.

Raay, Leon de, *The History of the Postage Stamps of the Orange Free State and Orange River Colony*. Amsterdam, 1907–1923.

PANAMA

Dumont, G. A., *Essai sur les Surcharges, 1903–1908*.

Heydon, F. E., *The Stamps of Panama*.

PAPUA AND NEW GUINEA (*see also* British Commonwealth)

Grosier, *Postmarks of Papua and New Guinea to 1943*.

PARAGUAY

Bose, Walter B. L., *Evolución del Correo en el Paraguay*.

Jewell, Charles, *Paraguayan War of 1864–1869 and Postal Services*.

Phillips, Charles J., *Stamps of Paraguay*. 1912.

PERSIA

Beckton, W. D., *The Barre Impressions of the 1868 Issue*.

———, *Notes on the Reprints of the Lion Issue*.

Dadkhan, *The Lion Stamps*. 1960.

Schuller, Friedrich, *Persien und Buchara Postwertzeichen*.

PERU

Lamy, Georges, *Study of Cancellations of 1857–1873.* 1960.

———, *Study of Postal Administration from 1857–1873.*

———, *Timbres et Obliterations de la Comp. de Navigation de L'Océan Pacifique.*

Moll, Herbert H., *Specialized Catalogue of Peru.*

Rommel, Otto, *Studien über die Postwertzeichen von Peru.*

Wickersham, C. W., *1860 Lithographs of Peru.*

PHILIPPINES

Bartels, John M., and others, *Postage Stamps of the Philippines.* Boston, 1904.

Marco, José E., *The Postage Stamps of the Philippine Islands, 1854–1899.* Bacolod, 1927.

POLAND

Mikstein and Rachmanov, W. von, *Stemple Pocztowe Ksiestwa Warszawskiego i Krolestwa Pols. 1808–1870.* 1938.

Polanski, W. von, and Rachmanov, W. von, *Die Postwertzeichen and Postempel von Polen im 18 und 19 Jahrhundert.* Vienna, 1935.

PORTUGAL AND PORTUGUESE COLONIES

Cunha Lamas, José da, *Estudio das Reimpressoes do Selos Portugueses.* Lisbon, 1948.

Ferreira, A. Simoes, *Imprimes en relief, 1852–1893.*

Fragoso, Antonio, *100 Anos do Selo do Correio Portugues.* Lisbon, 1953.

Harrison, Gilbert, and Napier, Francis J. H. S., *Portuguese India.* London, 1893.

Salvi, Constantino, *Postmarks of Portugal.*

PUERTO RICO

Monge, *Matasellos Españoles de Puerto Rico.*

Preston, R. B., and Sanborn, M. H., *The Postal History of Puerto Rico.* Federalsburg, Md., 1950.

QUEENSLAND (*see also* British Commonwealth)

Hull, Arthur F. B., *The Postage Stamps, Envelopes, Wrappers, Postcards and Telegraph Forms of Queensland.* London, 1930.

Porter, Harry S., *Queensland Numeral Cancellations.* 1954.

REUNION

Pomyers, Comte Olivier de, *Les Timbres de la Réunion, 1851–1939*. 1953.

RHODESIA (*see also* British Commonwealth)

Dann, H. C., *The Cancellations of the Rhodesias and Nyasaland*. London, 1940.

———, *The Romance of the Posts of Rhodesia, British Central Africa and Nyasaland*. London, 1950.

ROMANIA

Birnbach, Heinrich, *Die Rekonstruktion der Ausgaben, 1866–1872*.

———, *Moldau Walachei, Die Fremden und Einheimischen Posten bis 1875*.

Cohen, Eduardo, *Les Timbres de Roumanie des Emissions de 1872–1879*. Lisbon, 1952.

Racoviceanu, Gr., *Stampilele Postale Folosite in Tarile Romine Pina in Amul 1881*. 1963.

Tebeica, Val., *Les Premiers Timbres-Poste Roumains 1858–1865*. Bucharest, 1962.

Wilson, *Romania: 1866–1872 Issues Study*.

RUSSIA

Aronson and Savitzky, *Russian Aerophilately*.

Chuchin, F. G., *Catalogue of the Russian Rural Postage Stamps*. Moscow, 1925.

Herrick, William, *Catalogue of the Russian Rural Stamps*. 1896.

Romeko, *Catalogue Special des Timbres-Poste de Russie et des Etats Issue de l'Ancien Empire Russe*. 1927.

Schmidt, Carl, and Faberge, Agathon, *Die Postwertzeichen der Russischen Landschaftsämter*. Vol. I, Petrograd (undated) and Vol. II, Dresden, 1934.

Tchilinghirian, S. D., and Stephen, W. S. E., *Stamps of the Russian Empire Used Abroad*, Part IV. Ulan Bator, 1959.

RYUKYU ISLANDS

Sera, Minoru, *Ryukyus Handbook—Philatelic and Historic*. Tokyo, 1962.

SALVADOR

Berthold, Dr. Victor M., *1879 Issues, Including Plating*.

———, *Surcharges of 1889*.

———, *Forgeries of 1905–1906*.

SAMOA (*see also* British Commonwealth)

Yardley, Robert B., *The Samoa Express Postage Stamps.* London, 1916.

SARAWAK (*see also* British Commonwealth)

Hansford, G. E., and Noble, L. A., *Sarawak and Her Stamps.* London, 1935.

Poole, B. W. H., *The History and Postage Stamps of Sarawak.*

Wood, Forrester, *Sarawak Stamps and Postal History.* Redhill, England, 1959.

SERBIA

Derocco, E., *Serbia: Stamps, Cancellations and Postal Stationery, 1840–1921.*

SEYCHELLES (*see also* British Commonwealth)

Farmer, H. V., *Seychelles Postage Stamps and Postal History.* London, 1955.

SIAM

Linneman, Henry S., *Postal Stationery of Siam, 1883–1935.*

Siam Philatelic Society, *Descriptive Catalogue of the Postage Stamps and the Post and Letter Cards of Siam, 1883–1919.* Bangkok, 1920.

Toppan, *Siam, Stamps and Varieties.*

SOUTH AFRICA (*see also* British Commonwealth)

Rich, Stephen G., *Philately of the Anglo-Boer War, 1899–1902.*

Ward, Gordon, *The Ship Penny Stamp of South Africa.*

———, *The Springbok Half-Penny.* London, 1956.

SOUTH AUSTRALIA (*see also* British Commonwealth)

Philatelic Society of South Australia, *The Postage Stamps of South Australia.* Adelaide, 1952.

SOUTHWEST AFRICA (*see also* British Commonwealth)

Gewande, Herbert Werner, *Suedwest Afrika.* 1955.

Hoffman, Gieseche G., *Suedwestafrika.* 1966.

SPAIN AND SPANISH COLONIES

Aguilar, E. F., *Manuel del Experto, 1850–1900.* 1960.

Carreras, Francisco, *El Donativo Thebussem a la Biblioteca-Museo-Belaguer.*

———, *Tarjetas Postales.*

Carreras and Monge, *Sellos de Colegios de Escribanos de España, 1787–1862.* 1923.

Friedrich, Rudolf, *Die Postwertzeichen Spaniens und seiner Kolonien.* Berlin, 1894.

Griebert, Hugo, *The Stamps of Spain, 1850–1854.* London, 1919.

Guezala Ayrivie, Antonio de, *6 Cuartos 1850.* Bilbao, 1936.

Lenze, *Matesellos de Fecha en España, 1850–1865.*

Monge, Pedro, *Estudio de los Sellos Fiscales Españoles, 1637–1871.* 1923.

Thebussem, Dr., *Fruslerías Postales.* 1895.

Tort Nicolau, Arturo, *Guía del Coleccionista de Sellos de Correos de España, 1850–1900.* Reus, 1950–55.

STRAITS SETTLEMENTS (*see also* British Commonwealth)

Brown, William, *A Reference List to the Stamps of the Straits Settlements, Surcharged for Use in the Native Protected States.* Salisbury, 1894.

Wood, F. E., *Straits Settlements Postage Stamps.* Bettws-y-Coed, Wales, 1948.

SUDAN (*see also* British Commonwealth)

Gisburn, Harold G. D., and Thompson, G. Seymour, *The Stamps and Posts of the Anglo-Egyptian Sudan.*

SWEDEN

Forsell, Nils, *Svenska Postverkets Historia.* Stockholm, 1936.

Kungl. Generalpoststyrelsen, *Svenskt Postväsen.* Stockholm, 1924.

Lilliehook, *Helsakerna, 1872–1941.*

Menzinsky, Georg, *Postage Stamps of Sweden, 1920–1946.* Stockholm, 1946.

Nylander, Y., *Sveriges Fasts Postanstalter Genom Tiderna.* Stockholm, 1949.

Swedish Philatelic Society, *Handbok over Sveriges Frankoteckekn, 1855–1946.* Stockholm, 1946.

Thunaeus, *Militarbrev och Portofrihetsmarken.* 1946.

SWITZERLAND

Andres, F. X., and Emmenegger, Hans, *Grosses Handbuch der Abstempelungen auf Schweizer Marken, 1843–1882.* Lucerne, 1931.

Bertrand, Gustave, *Memorial Philatélique,* Vol. III, *Luxembourg, Switzerland and Liechtenstein.* Montpelier, 1934.

Henrioud, Marc, and Winkler, Jean J., *Les Marques Postales de la Suisse*. Bern, 1945.

Lininger, *Marques Postales de la Suisse Romande*. 1955.

Mirabaud, Paul, and Reuterskiöld, Axel de, *Les Timbres Poste Suisse, 1843–1862*. Paris, 1898.

Weber, H. Jaggli, *The Swiss Postmarks and Postal Cancellations, 1843–1862*. Lucerne, 1920.

TASMANIA (*see also* British Commonwealth and Australia)

Hull, Arthur F. B., *The Stamps of Tasmania*. London, 1890.

Royal Philatelic Society of Victoria, *Tasmania: The Postal History and Postal Markings*. Melbourne, 1962.

TIBET

Haverbeck, Harrison D. S., *The Potage Stamps and Postal History of Tibet*. New York, 1958.

Lobdell, H. E., *Indian Post Offices Abroad in Tibet*.

Radgowski, *Hand-Typographed Stamps of Tibet*.

TRANSVAAL (*see also* British Commonwealth)

Curle, J. H., and Basden, A. E., *Transvaal Postage Stamps*. London, 1940.

TUNISIA

Chapier, Georges, *Obliterations de Tunisie*. 1936.

Pomyers, Comte Olivier de, *Les Timbres de Tunisie, 1849–1888*.

TURKEY

Friedman, *Weltkrieg 1914–1915 und Philatelie*.

Neulinger, *Spezial Aufstellung der Turkischen Lokalpost-Marken*.

Passer, Adolf, *The Stamps of Turkey*. London, 1938.

Titze, *History of the Anatolia Postage Stamps*.

Tomkins, Maj. T. L. C., *Cancellations of Turkish Arabia*. 1956.

UKRAINE

Greaves and Roberts, *The Trident Issues of the Ukraine*. Winchcombe, 1953.

UNITED NATIONS

Metall, Dr. Rudolf A., *Postage Stamps and Postal Stationery of the United Nations*. New York, 1965.

UNITED STATES

Ashbrook, Stanley B., *Types & Plates of the United States One Cent Stamp of 1851–1857*. New York, 1926.

————, *The United States Ten Cent Stamp of 1855–1857*. New York, 1936.

————, *The United States Twelve Cent Stamp of 1851–1857*.

Blake, Maurice C., and Davis, Wilbur W., *Postal Markings of Boston, Massachusetts, to 1890*. Portland, 1949.

Boggs, Winthrop S., *Early American Perforating Machines and Perforations, 1857–1867*.

Brazer, Clarence W., *Essays for U. S. Adhesive Postage Stamps*. 1941.

Brookman, Lester G., *The 19th Century Postage Stamps of the United States*. New York, 1947.

Chase, Carroll, *The 3c Stamps of the United States, 1851–1857 Issue*. Springfield, Mass., 1942.

Chase, Carroll, and Cabeen, R. McP., *The First Hundred Years of United States Territorial Postmarks, 1787–1887*. 1950.

Conkling, Roscoe P., and Margaret B., *The Butterfield Overland Mail, 1857–1869*. Glendale, Calif., 1947.

Coster, Charles H., *Les Postes Privées des Etats-Unis d'Amérique*. Brussels, 1882–1885.

Couch, *Postal History of Alaska*. 1957.

Diamond, Alfred, and Kenworthy, Waldo V., *The United States One Cent Issues of 1851–1857*. Ord, Nebraska.

Dow, Sterling T., *Maine Postal History and Postmarks*. Portland, 1943.

Glass, Sol, *United States Postage Stamps, 1845–1852*. New York, 1954.

Goodkind, Henry M., *The 24c Air Mail Inverted Center of 1918*. New York, 1956.

————, *R. F. (French) Overprints 1944–45 on Air Mail Stamps*. New York, 1958.

————, *The 5c Beacon Air Mail Stamp of 1928*. New York, 1965.

Hafen, Le Roy R., *The Overland Mail, 1849–1869*. Cleveland, 1926.

Hahn, Mannel, *U. S. Postal Markings, 1847–1851*.

Hennan, Dr. Clarence A., *The Private Posts of Chicago*.

Hesly, Edward, and Diamond, Alfred, *The Types and Varieties of the United States Ten Cent Issues of 1855–1859*.

Huber, Leonard V., and Wagner, Clarence A., *The Great Mail*. 1949.

Johl, Max G., *The United States Commemorative Stamps of the Twentieth Century*. New York, 1947.

Kelly, M. Clyde, *United States Postal Policy*. New York, 1932.

King, Beverly S., and Johl, Max G., *The United States Stamps of the Twentieth Century*. New York, 1934–38.

Klein, Eugene, *United States Waterway Packetmarks*. 1940.

Long, Bryant A., and Dennis, William J., *Mail by Rail*. New York, 1951.

Loso, Foster W., and de Windt, Heyliger, *Twentieth Century United States Fancy and Topical Cancellations*. Elizabeth, N. J., 1952.

Luff, John N., *The Postage Stamps of the United States*. New York, 1937.

———, *United States Postmaster Provisionals*. New York, 1937.

Mueller, Barbara R., *United States Postage Stamps*. Princeton, N. J., 1958.

Mynchenberg, G. C., and Trout, Horace Q., *The Noble Official Catalog of United States Bureau Precancels*. 1966.

Neinken, Mortimer L., *The United States Ten Cent Stamps of 1855–1859*. New York, 1960.

Norona, Delf, *A Cyclopedia of United States Postmarks and Postal History*. Chicago, 1941.

Patton, Donald S., *Boyd's Local Posts in New York City, 1844–1882*. London.

———, *The Local Posts of Brooklyn, New York*. London.

Philatelic Research Laboratories, *The Edward S. Knapp Collection: Philatelic Americana*. New York, 1941.

Remele, C. W., *U. S. Railroad Postmarks, 1837–1861*. 1958.

Rees, James, *Foot-Prints of a Letter Carrier*. Philadelphia, 1866.

Rich, Wesley E., *The History of the United States Post Office to the Year 1829*. Cambridge, Mass., 1924.

Sampson, E. N., *The American Stampless Cover Catalog*. Albany, Ore., 1965.

Slater, A. B., *The Stamps of the Providence, R. I. Postmaster, 1846–1847*. Providence, 1930.

Stark, John S., and Boerger, Alfred G., *Luminescent United States Postage Stamps*. Ord, Neb., 1965.

Stern, Edward, *History of the "Free Franking" of Mail in the United States*. New York, 1936.

Thomas, William K., *History and Evolution of Metered Postage*. 1962.

Thorp, Prescott H., *Thorp-Bartels Catalogue of United States Stamped Envelopes.* Netcong, N. J., 1954.

Toppan, George L., and others, *An Historical Reference List of the Revenue Stamps of the United States.* Boston, 1899.

Van Lint, *United States Perfins.* 1958.

Winther, Oscar O., *Via Western Express and Stage Coach.* Stanford, 1945.

Zareski, Michel, and Herst, Herman, Jr., *Fancy Cancellations on 19th Century United States Postage Stamps.* Shrub Oak, N. Y., 1951.

Confederate States

Antrim, Earl, *Civil War Prisons and Their Covers.* 1961.

Dietz, August, *The Postal Service of the Confederate States of America.* Richmond, Va., 1929.

Laurence, Robert, *The George Walcott Collection of Used Civil War Patriotic Covers.*

Lehman, Howard, *Confederate States of America—The Two Cent Green Stamp.* New York, 1961.

Malpass, George N., *The Jefferson Davis Postage Stamp Issues of the Confederacy.* 1961.

Shenfield, Lawrence Ł., *Confederate States of America— Special Postal Routes.* 1961.

Hawaii

Crocker, Henry J., *Hawaiian Numerals.* San Francisco, 1909.

Davel and Spellman, *Hawaii Forgeries.*

Meyer, Henry A., and others, *Hawaii: Its Stamps and Postal History.* New York, 1948.

URUGUAY

Hoffmann, Roberto, *Catálogo de las Variedades más Importantes de los Sellos Postales de la República Oriental del Uruguay.* Santa Fé, Argentina, 1948.

————, *Estudio de las Falsificaciones de los Sellos Postales del Uruguay.* Montevideo, 1948.

Lee, Emanuel J., *The Postage Stamps of Uruguay.* London, 1931.

VENEZUELA

Hall, Thomas W., and Fulcher, L. W., *The Postage Stamps of Venezuela.* London, 1924.

Ron, S. W., *Origins of the First Stamps of Venezuela.* Caracas, 1958.

Wickersham, C. W., *The Early Stamps of Venezuela.* New York, 1958.

VICTORIA (*see also* British Commonwealth)

Pack, Charles L., *Victoria: The Half-Length Portaits and the Twopence Queen Enthroned.* New York, 1923.

Purves, James R. W., *The Half-Lengths of Victoria.* London, 1953.

————, *Barred Oval Cancellations, 1851–1856.* 1949.

————, *Victorian Butterfly Postmarks.* 1949.

————, *Victoria: The "Barred Numeral" Cancellations, 1856–1912.* Melbourne, 1963.

VIRGIN ISLANDS (*see also* British Commonwealth)

Dalwick, R. E. R., *Virgin Islands Handbook.*

CHAPTER 10

Postage Stamp Design: Prominent Americans Stamps of 1966

EVERY YEAR the Postmaster General's office is the recipient of hundreds of requests for and suggestions about new stamps. Right now there is a backlog of more than 3,000 such requests and suggestions awaiting final disposition. Their sources are many and varied—from any number of organizations that have figured prominently in American cultural, artistic, scientific, religious, or political life; from private citizens; from local branches of government; from Congress itself.

Each year the Postmaster General approves about fifteen commemorative themes for which artists throughout the country and within the Bureau of Engraving and Printing submit postage-stamp designs. He has ultimate authority to accept or reject them.

In the discharge of his duties as arbiter of choice of commemorative theme and stamp design to portray it, he has the assistance of the Citizens' Stamp Advisory Committee whose members he appoints. Members currently serving are: Reuben K. Barrick, Bureau of Engraving and Printing; Stevan

Dohanos, commercial illustrator and stamp designer; Belmont Faries, news editor and stamp editor of the Washington *Star;* Roger Kent, San Francisco attorney and philatelist; David Lidman, makeup editor of *The New York Times* and its stamp-column editor; Dr. James J. Matejka, Jr., Chicago physician and philatelist; Dr. Elsie M. Lewis, professor of history, Howard University; Roger L. Stevens, Special Assistant to the President on the Arts; Norman Todhunter, art director for a New York advertising agency; John Walker, director of the National Gallery of Art, Washington, D. C.; Kurt Wiener, graphic arts expert. Mr. Lidman serves as Chairman; Mrs. Virginia Brizendine, Director of Philately and Special Assistant to the Postmaster General, as Executive Secretary.

The Committee meets about four times a year in Washington, D. C., to review proposals and submit its own list of suggestions to the Postmaster General. It also reviews designs in progress and works actively with artists and designers as they move toward the finished stamp design and ultimate approval of it by the Postmaster General.

The following pages are a close look at the 1966 issues of the Prominent Americans series with emphasis on how the designer meets the challenge of creating a new postage stamp.

The Mathew Brady photograph, taken shortly before Lincoln met General Grant for the first time, the source of the stamp design

Bill Hyde, the designer of the Washington and Lincoln stamps

Design by Joe Cleary

Design by
Larry Redag

The 4c Lincoln stamp

Lincoln

THE ABRAHAM LINCOLN 4c stamp was issued November 19, 1965, as the first of the new regular postage series. The corresponding 4c coil stamp was issued May 28, 1966, at Springfield, Illinois, during the Lincoln Society of Philately convention.

Wilbur Rundles (Bill) Hyde, the designer of the 4c Lincoln stamp, was born in Indianapolis, Indiana. He grew up in Cleveland, Ohio, and studied at the Cleveland School of Art. More recently he attended the California College of Arts and Crafts classes in metal sculpture.

Bill Hyde is a freelance graphic designer with a studio in San Francisco, California. He is a member of the Society of Typographic Arts, Chicago, the San Francisco Artists and Art Directors Club, and the Illustrators Club of San Francisco. Since 1948 he has received awards every year from one or more of the advertising shows in major cities of the United States.

Concerning the design of the Lincoln stamp, Mr. Hyde wrote:

"In my home I have one of my sculptures, which says 'Preserve the old, but know the new.' This was the basic thinking as I worked on the Lincoln stamp.

"The portrait was based on one of the eight photographs taken by Mathew Brady February 9, 1865. Of these, there were four profiles known as the Brady profiles. This was one of them.

"The research took three weeks going through a dozen books, etc. Then I started making sketches. The first one started was a flag with the stars in a circle as a background behind Lincoln. On checking the correct flag to use, I found there were three flags used during Lincoln's presidency; also, that it is

forbidden to use a flag as a background, with someone or something in front of the flag. That killed that idea; and I'm glad it did, for it didn't specifically identify Lincoln. Any president could be placed in front of a flag.

"Incidentally, I wanted a background to identify Lincoln. The corner of the log cabin was drawn from a photograph of the cooperage where Lincoln studied as a young man in New Salem, Illinois. Basically, I wanted to show that a great man such as Lincoln started out in a very humble beginning and achieved the highest honor in his country."

Four San Francisco artists—Bill Hyde, Haines Hall, Joe Cleary and Larry Redag—submitted preliminary sketches for the Lincoln stamp, the first of the new "Prominent Americans" series. The Stamp Advisory Committee selected the design by Bill Hyde.

The engravers of the stamp were Joseph S. Creamer, Jr. (vignette), and George A. Payne (lettering). The stamps issued in panes of 100 are printed in unlimited quantity on the Cottrell press.

On the first day of sale in New York City 445,629 covers were canceled and 1,678,108 stamps were sold.

Onstot Residence and Cooper Shop, where Lincoln and his friend Isaac Onstot, oldest son of Henry Onstot, often studied together by the light of a fire kindled with the cooper's shavings. Here Lincoln perfected his knowledge of English with the help of Samuel Kirkham's "English Grammar." The background of the stamp shows a corner of this log cabin in the State Park, New Salem, Illinois.

Five designs submitted by Haines Hall

147

The stamp as issued

George Washington 5c

BILL HYDE's designs for the Washington stamp were first based on a portrait by Charles Fevret de Saint-Mémin. This portrait, done in 1798 by the young French artist, is believed to be the last Washington portrait. Mr. Hyde's comments accompany his designs:

"On the first design I submitted, I wanted a background to identify Washington. The design was returned because it was thought that Washington looked a little too old.

"I slightly changed the second design to have Washington look younger. Also I decided to heavy up his name and darken the background for contrast. Design was returned to me. The Stamp Advisory Committee thought that the Liberty Bell tied in with Benjamin Franklin more than Washington. (I still think that history shows Washington as the one single man who did more as a General of the Army, President of the Constitutional Committee and First President of the United States to bring about the freedom of our country.) Anyway, it was considered better that Washington should stand alone—something special as first President.

Bill Hyde's first designs were based on a portrait by Charles Fevret de Saint-Mémin.

These designs, developed from the Porthole Portrait, were not submitted to the Post Office.

Rembrandt Peale, Self-Portrait. [Courtesy New York Public Library]

"Porthole Portrait" by Rembrandt Peale. [Courtesy National Gallery of Art, Washington, D.C.]

"On the third design, I made the background plain and changed and simplified the lettering arrangement. This, I felt, made a very strong graphic design for a stamp. The Committee now wanted Washington to look older again, which was done. This third design was returned without comment, however. I suspect that because it was a profile, as was the Lincoln stamp, it was felt that it might be setting a precedent for the new 'Prominent Americans' series.

Design accepted with minor changes in lettering and background

"The Committee sent me a photograph of Rembrandt Peale's 'Porthole Portrait' and instructed me to build a new design around that. Two new designs were made using a half-tone photograph of this portrait. I was not satisfied with these two—they seemed ordinary and dull, and I decided not to submit them.

"The halftone photograph of the portrait was broken down to a black-and-white treatment which gave more contrast, making the design more graphic and interesting.

"This design was returned to me for changes in the lettering. Also, I decided to darken the background to bring out the top and sides of the head."

149

Robert L. Miller submitted three designs using Gilbert Stuart portraits.

Rejected design by Howard Mildner

Rembrandt Peale was one of the four sons of Charles Willson Peale. Through his father's influence he was permitted, at the age of seventeen, to paint Washington in Philadelphia in September, 1795. The old General granted the young artist three three-hour sittings. During his life Rembrandt Peale duplicated this portrait with variations 79 times.

The "Porthole Portrait" was painted in 1823, and it represents a combination of what the artist considered the best features of his first portrait and of several portraits painted by his father and by John Trumbull. He also used the study for the statue by Jean Antoine Houdon. The painting was bought by Congress in 1832 for $2,000 and now hangs in the office of Vice President Hubert H. Humphrey. Bill Hyde used as his working model a copy of this portrait, given to the National Gallery of Art, Washington, D. C., in 1942 by Mr. and Mrs. George W. Davison of New York City.

The 5c Washington in the "Prominent Americans" series, was released on Washington's Birthday, February 22, 1966. Bill Hyde designed the Washington stamp as well as the 4c Lincoln stamp. Bureau engraver Charles A. Brooks did the vignette, and William R. Burnell the lettering. The stamp was also released as a coil stamp September 8, 1966, in Cincinnati, Ohio, during opening ceremonies of the Philatelic Society convention.

Four designs were submitted by artists of the Bureau of Engraving and Printing, Howard C. Mildner and Robert L. Jones. There were 525,372 first-day cancellations, and 825,586 stamps were sold when the stamp went on sale in Washington, D. C.

The 6c Roosevelt stamp as issued

Franklin D. Roosevelt

FRANKLIN DELANO ROOSEVELT, thirty-second President of the United States, appears for the first time on a regular issue, the 6c stamp, issued at the St. James Parish House, Hyde Park, New York, January 29, 1966, the eighty-fourth anniversary of his birth.

Richard Lyon Clark, the designer of this stamp, searching through the files of the New York Public Library, of the Associated Press, and of *Life* Magazine, looked at about 1,500 photographs. He finally chose a World War II group photograph of Roosevelt, Winston S. Churchill, Admiral Ernest King and Admiral Harold R. Stark. However, for the design of the stamp, he turned FDR's head. An unidentified British official staff photographer took this picture aboard the British battleship *Prince of Wales,* off the coast of Newfoundland, August 15, 1941, one day after the signing of the Atlantic Charter.

Clark chose this particular photograph because it "depicts FDR with warmth, strength and optimism, and shows just the right tilt of the chin. The deep brown color was chosen because it suggests earth, reality, and the truth of simple things.

Preliminary sketches made, according to Mr. Clark, ". . . to give me a feeling of positioning the portrait of Mr. Roosevelt and of the type. These are rough idea sketches and were a means of exploring design possibilities."

"The type is Franklin Gothic and is unobtrusive in order not to distract from the portrait. It forms a background in a somewhat sculptural sense to the

Photograph taken August 15, 1941, the source of the portrait

Richard Lyon Clark, the designer of the stamp

face of Mr. Roosevelt. The numeral is placed in an isolated but prominent spot to identify the denomination quickly."

Richard Lyon Clark is a native of San Diego, and a graduate of the Art Center School of Los Angeles. He is now an art director with a New York advertising firm and lives in Connecticut.

As a youth, Dick Clark painted water colors of the yachts moored in San Diego Bay and sold them to the skippers, who encouraged him to study art and to make it his career. Growing up close to the ocean, he became an expert fisherman and earned his tuition for art school by tuna fishing off the coast of Mexico.

After graduation, he was asked to teach at the Art Center School. Since then he has switched to advertising, working in this field in Los Angeles, Chicago, Detroit and New York.

Joseph S. Creamer, Jr., engraved the portrait and Howard Sharpless the lettering. Both are with the Bureau of Engraving and Printing. The stamps are issued in panes of 100; the printing order is unlimited. On the first day of sale in New Hyde Park, 877,500 stamps were sold, and 448,631 first-day covers were canceled.

These two preliminary designs were rejected by artist Clark himself because he felt they were not as characteristic of the warmth and strength of FDR as the design finally chosen.

Three designs submitted by staff artists of the Bureau of Engraving and Printing. From left to right, the designs are by Robert L. Miller, Robert J. Jones and Howard C. Mildner.

The stamp as issued

Albert Einstein

ALBERT EINSTEIN is the "Prominent American" selected for the 8c stamp issued March 14 at Princeton, New Jersey. Einstein was born in Ulm, Germany, in 1879; he studied in Germany and Switzerland.

He published his first paper concerning the theory of relativity in 1905. When thirty years old, Einstein was appointed Director of the Kaiser-Wilhelm Physical Institute in Berlin. He received the Nobel Prize in Physics in 1921.

While Einstein was lecturing in Pasadena, California, in 1932, he was invited to join the newly founded Institute for Advanced Studies at Princeton. He accepted and became the first member of the Institute's staff. Originally he had planned to divide his time equally between his duties in Berlin, Germany, and Princeton. After Hitler came to power in Germany in 1933, Einstein made his permanent home in Princeton, where he stayed until his death in 1955.

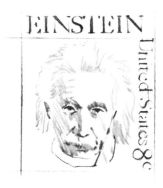

In 1939 Einstein wrote President Roosevelt warning about the possibilities of nuclear fission and about the advances in these studies in Germany. As a result, the United States embarked on the Manhattan Project, which developed the atom bomb.

Frank Sebastiano, the designer of the Einstein stamp, is art director for a New York advertising firm, and is also a stamp collector. He studied at the Ontario College of Art in Toronto and with the Art Students League. Previously, in 1965, he designed the Battle of New Orleans stamp. Mr. Sebastiano

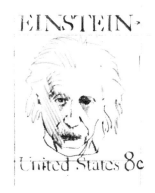

Three preliminary pencil sketches by Frank Sebastiano

153

Frank Sebastiano

Philippe Halsman photographed by his wife Yvonne

chose a photograph by Philippe Halsman for the portrait on the stamp and used a Caslon type for the lettering.

Philippe Halsman, the photographer, was named one of the world's ten great photographers at an international poll in 1958. Halsman was born in Latvia and studied engineering in Germany. Later, he moved to France and, having been an amateur photographer, opened a portrait studio in Paris. He came to the U.S. in 1940 and within four years he became the first president of the American Society of Magazine Photographers. Mr. Halsman is a member of the Guiding Faculty of the Famous Photographers School in Westport, Connecticut. Though he is best known for his portraits (his portrait of Adlai Stevenson appears on the 1965 stamp), Halsman also does much illustrative work and contributes to many magazines.

Halsman tells the following story concerning the origin of the Einstein photograph. After the fall of France in 1940, Professor Einstein secured an emergency visa for Halsman and his French wife, which permitted them to come to the United States. When he visited the professor at Princeton to thank him for his help, Halsman, knowing Einstein's dislike of being photographed, did not ask him to pose for him at that time.

On May 10, 1947, Halsman again visited Einstein in his home. This time he happened to have with him a large camera and a few lights. Einstein consented to have his picture taken and allotted Halsman a half-hour in his study. As he posed, Einstein spoke of his unhappiness to see atomic energy, whose release stemmed from his theory of relativity, being used for the manufacture of atom bombs. Halsman recalls that when Einstein was shown the

print and asked if he liked it, he replied, "Well, I dislike it less than the others."

Albert Einstein's portrait first appeared on a stamp of Israel in 1956. When Germany released her "Famous Germans" series in 1961, it was planned to have Einstein on the two-mark stamp. The Einstein family, however, refused to grant permission.

Arthur W. Dintaman and George A. Payne of the Bureau of Engraving and Printing engraved the stamp. There were 366,803 first-day covers canceled, and 613,204 stamps sold on the first day of issue.

Israel's Einstein stamp

 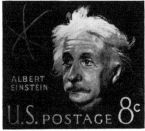 

Three designs prepared by artists of the Bureau of Engraving and Printing. Robert J. Jones's design (left) and Robert L. Miller's used the same photograph. Howard C. Mildner added an atom symbol in the background.

The Solomon R. Guggenheim Museum, interior view [Courtesy The Solomon R. Guggenheim Museum]

Design by Victor S. McCloskey, Jr.

Profile portrait adapted by Mr. and Mrs. Vernon Swabeck

David Wheatley used geometrical lines, symbolic of Taliesin West, as background.

156

Ling Po framed portrait with brick arch

The stamp as issued

Frank Lloyd Wright

FRANK LLOYD WRIGHT, the architect, was a man of vision and ideas, a creator and pathfinder. His ideas were scorned, ridiculed, and finally imitated.

He was ahead of his time when as a young man he conceived the idea of the "natural house," a dwelling which not only fits into its surroundings but which also would be functional to the needs of its occupants. He was still ahead of his time when he designed the Guggenheim Museum in New York City, shortly before his death in 1959 at the age of ninety. One of his greatest triumphs, not only as an architect but also as an engineer, was the Imperial Hotel in Tokyo. The Emperor officially invited Frank Lloyd Wright in 1916 to build a hotel in Tokyo which would serve the growing number of foreign visitors and businessmen. The hotel that Mr. Wright designed, and which he personally helped build, perfectly blended Western comfort with Japanese style. The materials were Japanese, the technique American. More important, however, than the style was the fact that the hotel was designed to withstand earthquakes. This building proved beyond all expectations the genius of its builder when it withstood the horrible earthquake of September 1923, which destroyed most of Tokyo and all its large buildings.

The S. C. Johnson & Son Administration Building in Racine, Wisconsin, built in 1939, and the Research Tower, built in 1950, showed a new concept in office buildings. Many of Wright's innovations in building private homes have become regular features in contemporary buildings. He transformed the "parlor" into the "living room" and introduced indirect lighting, radiant heat and the indoors-outdoors living area.

The Solomon R. Guggenheim Museum, New York City. View from Fifth Avenue [Courtesy The Solomon R. Guggenheim Museum]

New York's Guggenheim Museum, shown in the background of the 2c stamp released June 8, 1966, was opened October 21, 1959, five months after Frank Lloyd Wright's death. He patterned the building after the spiral of a seashell. The visitors walk along a gently rising ramp past the exhibits without interruptions. Like all other works by Mr. Wright, the building was controversial, but as time went by it blended into its surroundings and has become a great tourist attraction on upper Fifth Avenue in New York City.

Design from which accepted design was developed

In 1932 he announced his intention to train architects in a working community at his home, Taliesin, in Spring Green, Wisconsin. From this beginning grew Taliesin West, a workshop at Scottsdale, Arizona, established by the Frank Lloyd Wright Foundation.

Design by Robert J. Jones

The design of this stamp in the series was a joint project of members of the staff at Taliesin West, under the guidance of his widow Olgivanna Wright. Patricia Armantides, a native of Rochester, New York, drew the portrait after a photograph by Blackstone-Shelburne of New York City. A Chinese artist, Mr. Ling Po, drew the museum, and John Armantides and Vernon Swaback did the lettering and background.

A team of artists at Taliesin West submitted four variations of the accepted design and also additional designs using different portraits. Members of the Bureau of Engraving and Printing also were asked to submit designs.

Josef Fabris added outlines of Guggenheim Museum and of Price Tower to full-face portrait.

Howard C. Mildner, Arthur W. Dintaman (vignette) and Kenneth C. Wiram (lettering) of the Bureau prepared the master die. On the first day of issue in Spring Green, Wisconsin, 1,421,864 stamps were sold and 460,427 covers were canceled.

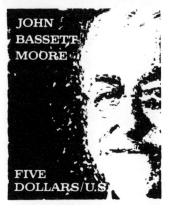

FIVE DOLLARS/U.S.

Advance photo of the final design made available by the Post Office Department prior to the first day of issue

John Bassett Moore

THE HIGHEST DENOMINATION, $5, of the series was released December 3, 1966, in Smyrna, Delaware. John Bassett Moore, honored with this stamp, was born there on that date 106 years ago.

He became Third Assistant Secretary of State at twenty-five, although he had only attended, but never graduated from, the University of Virginia. He went on to become the foremost authority of his day on international law, and Professor of International Law and Diplomacy at Columbia University from 1891 to 1924. His eight-volume work, *A Digest of International Law,* was published in 1906 and is still considered a basic textbook on the subject. He served this country on many international assignments such as the Conference on Samoan Affairs, the United States and Dominican Mixed Commission, the International Commission of Jurists, the Permanent Court of Arbitration in The Hague, and the Permanent Court of International Justice. During 1922–23 he was president of the International Conference on Rules for Aircraft and Radio in Time of War in The Hague. He died in 1947 in New York City.

Tom Laufer, of Sausalito, California, is a newcomer to stamp design, although he had previously submitted ideas for the SIPEX commemorative stamp. Mr. Laufer attended Cooper Union in New York City. He is a member of the Society of Typographic Arts and The International Center of Typographic Arts and is regional chairman of the International Design Conference in Aspen, Colorado. His work has appeared in U.S. and European

Tom Laufer

158

John Bassett Moore, 1930

publications, and his packages and trademarks are part of the "Design U.S.A." Exhibit in London. He has also exhibited in Europe and Japan and is the recipient of many awards for excellence in design.

The stamp design was chosen from six different sketches. It is based on a photograph that appeared in the *American Bar Association Journal* in September, 1946.

According to Tom Laufer, his aim was a simple, direct arrangement of the elements of the design, dignified and contemporary in layout.

The stamp was printed on the Cottrell press, and the engravers were Arthur W. Dintaman (vignette) and William R. Burnell (lettering). There were 41,130 covers canceled and 68,062 stamps sold on the first day of sale.

CHAPTER 11

Index of U.S. Stamp
Designers

An alphabetical listing of designers followed by the. Scott Catalogue number of the stamp or stamps for which they were responsible.

Adams, Clifton: 903
Allen, Douglas: 1247
Arno, Enrico: 1071

Baker, Robert: 1129
Baldwin, Marcus W.: 329, 372–373
Bayer, Herbert: 1319
Beall, Lester: 1119
Bencsath, Henry K.: 1206, C64–C65
Block, Herbert L.: 1312
Bobertz, Carl: 1155
Bode, Robert: 1317
Brackett, Ward: 1199
Briggs, Austin: C54
Brown, J. Carter: 1273
Buckley, William H.: 1096, 1110–1111, 1117–1118, 1120, 1123, 1125–1126, 1131, 1136–1137, 1147–1148, 1159–1160, 1164–1165, 1168–1169, 1174–1175, C51–C52, C60–C61

Carter, Charles Henry: 1135, 1316
Cary, George F., II: 1095
Chemi, James M.: 1192
Chickering, C. R.: 1017, 1019, 1021, 1027–1028, 1030–1031, 1033, 1035–1046, 1048–1055, 1057–1058, 1059A–1061, 1063, 1066–1067, 1069, 1073–1074, 1084, 1087, 1093, 1121, 1138, 1156–1157, 1168–

1169, 1171, 1177, 1178, 1183–1184, 1187–1189, 1193–1195, 1198, FA1

Christenson, B. Harold: 1181

Clark, Richard: 1284

Clarke, Rene: 1108

Coiner, Charles T.: 1163

Conley, Frank P.: 1105, 1139–1144

Copeland, Arnold: 1096, 1109–1111, 1117–1118, 1125–1126, 1131, 1136–1137, 1147–1148, 1159–1160, 1162, 1164–1166, 1174–1175

Crawford, Jim: 1205

Dias, Ronald: 1085

Dingee, Tyler: 1031A, 1054A

Dohanos, Stevan: 1127, 1132, 1153, 1231, 1263, 1320

Ermoyan, Suren H.: C56

Feher, Joseph: C55

Foster, Robert: 1134

Frasconi, Antonio: 1237

Fujikawa, Gyo: 1158, 1318

Gallatin, Robert: 1279

Geismar, Thomas H.: 1314

Geissmann, Robert: 1099, 1201

Genders, Richard J.: 1091

Gillen, Denver: 1100

Gjertson, Roy: 1180

Gorsline, Douglas: 1123, 1250, 1268

Goslin, George: 1119

Grafakos, Stella: 1315

Grove, E. R.: C48, C50

Giusti, George: 1112

Hallen, Ernest: 856

Hallock, Robert: 1124

Helguera, Leon: 907, 947, 1157

Hill, Homer: 1106

Hines, Bob: 1077–1079, 1098

Hortens, Walter: 1133

Hurd, Richard F.: 1264, 1272

Huston, C. Aubrey: 323–328, 330, 367–371, 397, 399, 401, 403, 537, 548–550, 611–615, 617–621, 627–630, 643–645, 649–651, 657, 680–683, 702–704, 706–708, 711, 713–714, 725–726, 856

Hyde, Bill: 1282–1283

Ihms, Jimmie E.: 1192

Jones, Robert J.: 1042A, 1208, 1235, 1244, 1261, 1276, 1322, C66, C68–C69

Klauck, Edward: 1309

Larrinague: 773
Laufer, Tom: 1295
Lea, Tom: 1242
Lewandowski, Edmund C.: 1313
Lockwood, Richard C.: C53
Loewy, Raymond/William Snaith, Inc.: 1246
Lomberdero, Joseph: C58–C59, C63
Lubalin, Herb: C58–C59, C63

Maas, John: 1151, 1185, 1196, 1270
Macdonough, James: 55–111, 113–114, 116–117, 121
MacEwen, Harold E.: 1088
Main, A. M., Jr.: 1095
Major, Alfred Saxoney: 230–245
Major, James Parsons: 1–4
Manship, Paul: 908
Marsh, Sam: 1267
Maulin, Gabriel: 852
McCloskey, Victor S.: 718–719, 724, 728–729, 732–735, 737–728, 740–764, 766–770, 772, 774, 778, 784, 787, 799, 800, 835–836, 898, 923–924, 928–930, 933, 935, 937, 939–942, 1018, 1029, 1039, 1045–1046, 1049, 1052–1053, 1059A, 1064, 1070, 1072, 1075, 1077–1079, 1081–1083, 1094, 1164, 1200, 1207, 1239, 1249, 1251, C47, C62, C67, E20–E21, FA1
Meissner, Alvin R.: 649, 654–656, 682, 683, 688–690, 702, 705, 709, 710, 712, 715–717, 724, 727, 736, 773, 775–778, 782–783, 790–795, 798, 838, 854, 858, 897, 903
Metzl, Ervine: 1095–1097, 1107, 1110–1111, 1113, 1114, 1115, 1117–1118, 1125–1126, 1131, 1136–1137, 1146–1149, 1159–1160, 1165–1166, 1168–1169, 1173–1175
Mildner, Howard C.: 1321
Miller, Robert L.: 1034, 1056, 1202, 1230, 1236, 1241, 1258
Morris, Thomas F.: 205, 210–229, 246–284
Mullen, Jerry: 1179, 1197
Mutchler, Dwight: 1232

Naegele, Thomas F.: 1254–1257, 1274, 1310
Nagy, Alexander: C49

O'Dea, Mark: 905
Olden, Georg: 1233
Oliver, H. Edward: 1167

Packard, Butler: 134, 204, 206–209
Parker, Alfred Charles: 1190
Parker, Jason S.: 629, 630
Petruccelli, Anthony: 1090
Pistilli, John: C58–C59, C63
Pitcher, E.: 112, 115, 118–120
Pollock, A. L.: 1131
Pringle, Bert: 1306
Purcell, Edward: 5–39

Rawlinson, Elaine: 803–834
Reaves, Logan U.: 924
Richards, Esther A.: 749, 765
Richards, Walter Dubois: 1290
Riley, Kenneth P.: 936
Roache, William A.: 796, 799, 801, 852, 855–856, 859–
    895, 899–901, 904–906, 922, 924–925, 934
Rockwell, Norman: 1145, 1238
Ross, John: 1259

Samerjan, George: 1128, 1275
Sanborn, Herbert M.: 1203–1204, 1266
Schick, L. E.: 789
Schmidt, Harold von: 1154
Schrage, William K.: 785–786, 788, 796, 857, 896, 931–
    932, 943–944, 1020, 1022–1023, 1025–1026, 1032,
    1044A, 1047, 1049, 1062, 1065, 1068–1069, 1075,
    1086, 1092, 1130, 1161, 1170, 1172, 1188, 1209,
    1213, 1225, 1229, 1234, 1243, 1248, C48, C62
Schultz, Robert J.: 1089
Sebastiano, Frank: 1285
Sickles, Noel: 1179
Sivard, Robert: 1152
Smith, R. Ostrander: 285–299
Spandorf, Lily: 1240
Stearn, J. R.: 798

Temple, Brook: 1265, 1271, 1311
Thompson, Bradbury: 1104, 1252
Todhunter, Norman: 1186, 1197, 1253, 1262, 1269, 1307

Trottier, Gerald: 1131

Wehr, Paul: 1308
Wendelin, Rudolph: 1122, 1176, 1245
White, Elmo: 1150
Willett, Emil J.: 1260
Winn, Buchanan: 938

Zorach, Mrs. William: 1095

CHAPTER 12

Questions and Answers

THE SCOTT MAIL BAG steadily disgorges a small Niagara of stamp queries. Many concern the listings or lack of listings in Scott's Standard and United States Specialized Catalogues. In the following selections from this constant flow of questions, you will probably find a few that have puzzled you, too.

Taboo on Red China, etc.

Q: Scott catalogues and albums list no stamps of North Viet Nam, Red China or North Korea, and none issued by Castro's Cuba since mid-1961. Stamps of these countries do turn up on commercial mail and occasionally I get a few. I'd like to have places for them in my albums and be able to look them up in Scott's Catalogue. Why aren't they listed?

—O. D. L., Pittsburgh.

One of the banned stamps of Communist Cuba—a three-colored 13c celebrating the third anniversary of the Bay of Pigs "victory." The falling dead eagle has a gunsight placed over his breast.

A: An act of the U.S. Treasury Department forbids Americans to import any product, including stamps, of these countries. It also forbids buying and selling of such stamps. Violators face possible fincs—even jail. The Catalogue editors prefer to support their government rather than encourage any illegal traffic in these issues by listing them. However, European-based catalogues do list and price

these forbidden stamps because their governments have issued no such embargo.

Misplaced Colors

Q: Many bicolored and multicolored stamps of the United States and other countries, particularly those of the past two decades, often have one color slightly or grossly out of place. I have searched the catalogues but cannot find any of these misprinted stamps listed.

—C. J. S., Richmond, Va.

This black and red 2c is often found with the Red Cross misaligned. The normal position for the red impression of the cross is at right.

A: On the older bicolored stamps printed with two plates on a flat-bed press, misalignment of the parts of a design printed in the second color frequently turns up. Stamps printed on high-speed rotary presses that apply two or more colors simultaneously sometimes show a bleeding of one color into areas intended for another. As both kinds of "misplaced color" are not constant (like a plate defect) and as both exist in endless degree, Catalogue editors cannot attempt to list them. Generally the editors can consider only the stamps on which one color is omitted or inverted.

Those Quarter Perforations

Q: The Bahamas 1959 commemoratives for their stamp centenary are perforated 13½—at least my

set is—but the Catalogue says they are "Perf. 13." The 1p is enclosed, if you care to measure it. Do I have unlisted varieties, or is the Catalogue wrong?
—P. H. D., Cleveland.

A: Bahamas Nos. 174-177 are actually perforated 13¼. The general catalogues, such as Scott's, do not measure in quarter perforations. When faced with a stamp measuring 13¼, the editors put it down as either 13 or 13½. The average perforation gauge gives only half perforations. One or two better gauges permit measurements to one-tenth of a point.

This stamp is actually perforated 13¼.

From Used to Mint

Q: I read recently in a stamp paper that it is possible to remove cancellations from used stamps and re-gum them to make them look mint. Where can I learn how to do this? Or where can I send my stamps to have this done?
—F. X. S., Chicago.

A: This, sir, constitutes fraud and is not recommended, even when done with the sole motive of making your stamps appear more attractive in the album. A reasonable amount of cleaning to remove soiled spots or stains and pressing to remove creases is certainly good, but the removal of cancellations and adding of gum are operations which cannot be condoned. Collectors who buy valuable stamps may first have them expertized to make sure that such dubious tampering and face-lifting have not been done.

Missing Catalogue Numbers

Q: I notice that there is no stamp listed for Jugo-slavia No. 626. Did this listing get dropped out of my Catalogue by accident?

—P. J. D., Wilton, Conn.

A: No stamp is missing in the Catalogue listings at this point. The editors were under the impression that another low denomination would be released later for the regular series, Nos. 627-645, and skipped a number to accommodate it when it turned up. But no such stamp was issued, so the vacant number remains.

Number gaps will be found in many countries throughout the Catalogue. These need not worry the Catalogue user. The numbers used are the ones that identify their respective stamps, so any missing numbers have no meaning as stamp tags.

Various reasons account for these missing numbers. Sometimes a stamp may be listed as a regular postage issue, but when later information indicates it was used only as a Postal Tax stamp, it has to be moved to the Postal Tax section with "RA" preceding the stamp numbers. This, of course, leaves a hole in the consecutive numbering.

When a nation issues a long, regular-postage, non-commemorative series over a several-year stretch without announcing in advance the number of stamps in the set and their denominations, the editors frequently have a difficult time keeping the numbering in hand. Compromises have to be made to avoid renumbering many stamps.

Straight Edges

Q: I have a number of U.S. stamps, including the 3c dull red of 1857, which have no perforations on one side. Are these worth more or less than similar stamps with perforations on four sides?

—F. S. O., Los Angeles.

A straight edge copy of the 3c of 1869.

A: The older U.S. issues, printed on flat-bed presses, have one or two sides of each pane, or post office sheet, which are imperforate. These occur as the panes are cut apart to divide the larger sheet, as printed, before the stamps reach the post office. The stamps with one side imperforate are called *straight edges*. Although they are far less numerous than the perf.-on-four-sides stamps, the straight edges generally sell for less because collectors prefer the balanced appearance of perforations all around.

Modern Foreign Imperforates

Q: I collect foreign stamps and have recently acquired imperforate sets from Sharjah, Hungary, Poland, Romania and a couple of other countries which are not listed in the Catalogue or Supplements. Why aren't they listed? And what are they worth?

—J. C., Houston.

In Hungary the government sells imperforate sets at four times face.

A: In some countries, the imperforate issues are simply a way of making more money by extra sales to collectors. The Catalogue note about Hungarian imperforates will help to explain the lack of listings:

Nearly all Hungarian stamps from No. 859 on were issued imperforate as well as with perforations. In most cases the imperforate quantities were smaller than the per-

forated ones. The imperforates were sold at five times face value, and all issued before Feb. 22, 1958, were invalid. Late in 1958, Philatelica Hungarica started selling the imperforates at four times face value.

The existence of some imperforates is reported in footnotes in the Scott Catalogue. Others such as those of France and Hungary are dealt with in general notes in the Catalogue.

It is not possible to make a general statement on the market value of unlisted imperforates.

This Spanish stamp is not in the Catalogue because it paid no postage, but represents a voluntary contribution "Por la Patria."

Revenues, Seals, Fantasies

Q: On my "To Be Identified" stock page, I have many stamps which I cannot find listed in the Catalogue. Some designs are similar to those listed. How can I learn what these stamps are? Why aren't they listed?

—S. J. Q., Milwaukee.

A: Only *postage* stamps get listed in Scott's Catalogue. The ones you are trying to identify may be revenues, charity seals, poster stamps or foreign envelope stamps which have been cut out of their wrapper or envelope. Or they could be bogus or phantom stamps.

If your friends at the local stamp club or your favorite dealer can't give you a positive identification, try writing to one of the study groups or specialists' societies listed elsewhere in this book. Possibly the Cinderella Stamp Club could help.

Colors Can Change

Q: I have two stamps whose colors do not match those given in the Catalogue. One is a lilac stamp

which is listed as being lilac and blue. The other is brown, but is listed as having been issued only in orange. Do I have new varieties of these stamps?

—J. P. M. Portland, Me.

A: The blue has probably faded away on the stamp that should be blue and lilac. Exposure to the sun or other strong light will sometimes do this. Your brown stamp seems to be an example of oxidation. It was printed in orange. Catalogues report only the colors of the stamps as issued.

Specializing in Cancels

Q: I have many covers with special cancellations —naval, first flight, flag, etc. They do not seem to be listed. How can I learn their value?

—S. H. S., Philadelphia.

A: Special cancellations are a tremendous field. Only a few are included, even in specialized catalogues. There are societies which may be able to help you determine the value of your covers. You will find them in the Philatelic Study Groups and Societies section of this book under the subheading "Cancellations and Postmarks."

Keeping Up to Date

Q: How can I keep up with new issues that have come out since the Catalogue was published?

—J. S. B., Toledo. O.

A: Scott's Monthly Stamp Journal carries a supplement to the Scott Catalogues in every issue. The

subscription address is: Scott Publications, Inc., 1255 Portland Place, Boulder, Colo. 80302. Rates: $4 a year in the U.S.; to Canada, $4.50; to other countries, $5.

Stampless Covers

Q: I have several folded letters of 1800–1845 with markings I cannot find mentioned in the Catalouge. They carry no stamps. One of these letters has a circular postmark, BOSTON PAID NOV. 22, in black. Could these be unlisted postmaster's provisionals? How much are they worth?

—D. P., Boston.

A: The items you describe are stampless covers (letters of the pre-stamp period), not postmaster's provisionals. Some stampless covers are fairly common (such as the Boston one you describe) and sell for about 50 cents. If yours all originated in the U.S., they can probably be found listed in The American Stampless Cover Catalog, edited by E. N. Sampson. These you have found could become the nucleus of an interesting collection limited to your state, city or locality.

The Bogy of Color

Q: Color names given in catalogues often conflict and confuse. There must be hundreds of names used in Scott, yet I am told that no color chart is available that might give uniformity to all the colors described in all the catalogues. Couldn't someone revise the color names and introduce a uniform system?

—J. D. A., St. Louis.

A: The Scott Catalogue has been published for a century. Over the years many editors have worked on them. Each editor had different color opinions. As you know, two persons seldom see the same color as exactly the same hue.

Names used for colors have also changed down the decades. "Lake," "puce" and "stone"—not to mention "flesh"—no longer evoke the same mental picture for today's collectors that they did for earlier generations.

Used stamps cannot serve in determining colors. In order to establish a uniform color system in the catalogues, it would be necessary to amass a complete mint collection of all listed stamps. You can easily see the impossibility. Also, a stamp seen in direct sunlight will appear to have a different color under artificial light. Printing methods also affect a stamp's color. A certain ink, when used for lithography, may not produce exactly the same color when used in engraving.

All these factors work to prevent uniform color nomenclature. Since colors are named in a catalogue primarily for identification, the general colors recorded (blue, green, red, etc.) are entirely satisfactory for most collectors.

Puzzling Part Perforate

Q: A used 6c U.S. airmail stamp, issued in 1943 (Scott No. C25), puzzles me. It is imperforate on both sides and the bottom. Could this be an unlisted coil which someone trimmed at the bottom? Or an unlisted imperforate which someone perforated at the top? Is it worth anything?

     —H. S. Q., St. Petersburg, Fla.

A: Your stamp is the bottom one of three in the booklet pane No. C25a. It is worth no more, and probably somewhat less, than a used 6c from the sheet, perforated on four sides.

Collection Value

Q: My collection contains more than 5,000 different stamps, mostly used and in good condition. Recently I tried to sell it, and although it catalogues at least $50, a dealer offered me only $7 for it. I got the stamps from packets and off mail. I know the dealer is not in business for his health, but surely my collection is worth more, isn't it?

—P. D. T., San Francisco.

A: Since you obtained your stamps from packets and mail, they are probably the commonest material on the market. Stamps of this type can be bought in packets of 5,000 or more for a low price; a dealer can buy them at wholesale. While the minimum catalogue price of a stamp is fixed at 2c or 3c to cover the dealer's labor and service cost of sorting, cataloguing and filling orders individually, the sum of these list prices does not properly represent the value of packet stamps or stamps sold in bulk, which generally are all cheaper stamps.

Is it logical for a dealer or another collector to pay you more for your collection than it would cost him to buy the same stamps from another source?

CHAPTER 13

Philatelic Agencies of the World

THE FOLLOWING LIST of Postal Administrations and Philatelic Agencies is provided for those who may wish to try to order new issues or first-day covers directly from the issuing government, rather than to buy them the easy way—from a dealer. It is only fair to point out that on small orders the cost of negotiable remittance, return postage and registration greatly exceeds the reasonable charge over face value made by most stamp dealers. Direct purchase may be reasonable for complete definitive issues, but not for commemorative sets of three or four low values. A response to an order sent to a remote colony may require weeks or even months to reach the collector.

Many foreign agencies circulate illustrated brochures with details about their forthcoming stamps. Often these may be obtained regularly by asking to be placed on the mailing list. Some philatelic agencies do not cater to the individual collector but sell only to dealers. The British Crown Agents, for example, will provide information on issues of the Commonwealth, but limit their sales to dealers. The collector must order directly from the stamp-issuing country or buy the stamps from his dealer.

Collectors should write to a foreign agency before

placing an order to learn that country's regulations governing the sale of its stamps. (Some governments accept international money orders as payment, while others require U.S. currency.) All correspondence should be via air mail.

Abu Dhabi—Postal Superintendent, British Postal Agencies, Bahrain, Arabian Gulf.

Aden—Postmaster, Aden Posts and Telegraph Department, Aden, Arabia.

Afghanistan—Director General of Posts, Kabul, Afghanistan.

Ajman—General Post Office, Ajman, Arabian Gulf (via Bahrain).

Albania—Exportal, Rue 4 Shkust, Tirana, Albania.

Algeria—Director of Posts, Algiers, Algeria.

Andorra (French)—Administration des Postes, Andorre-la-Vieille (via France).

Andorra (Spanish)—*see address under* Spain.

Angola—Postmaster, Luanda, Angola.

Antigua—Colonial Postmaster, St. Johns, Antigua, B.W.I.

Argentina—Ministry of Communications, Franqueo (B), Central Post Office, Buenos Aires, Argentina.

Ascension—Postmaster, G. P. O., Jamestown, St. Helena, South Atlantic, or Postmaster, Ascension Island, South Atlantic.

Australia—Director General of Posts and Telegraphs, Philatelic Bureau, G. P. O., Melbourne C2, Australia.

Austria—Philatelic Agency, Postgasse 8, Vienna 1, Austria.

Bahamas—Postmaster of Bahamas, Nassau, Bahamas.

Bahrain—Chief Postmaster, Manama, Bahrain, Arabian Gulf.

Barbados—Colonial Postmaster, G. P. O., Bridgetown, Barbados, B.W.I.

Basutoland—*see* Lesotho.

Bechuanaland Protectorate—*see* Botswana.

Belgium—Philatelic Service, Postal Administration, Place de la Monnaie, Brussels 1, Belgium.

Bermuda—Colonial Postmaster, Philatelic Branch, G. P. O., Hamilton, Bermuda.

Bhutan—Bhutan Trust, Ltd., P. O. Box 66, Nassau, Bahamas.

Bolivia—Philatelic Section, General Directorate of Posts, La Paz, Bolivia.

Botswana (ex-Bechuanaland Prot.)—Postmaster, Lobatsi, Botswana (via South Africa).

Brazil—Departmento Central de Correos é Telégrafos, Philatelic Section, Rua Visconde de Itaborai S/N, Terro, Rio de Janeiro, Brazil.

British Guiana—*see* Guyana.

British Honduras—Colonial Postmaster, G. P. O., Belize, British Honduras.

Brunei—Postmaster, Brunei, North Borneo.

Bulgaria—Raznoiznos, State Commercial Enterprise, 1 Tsar Assen St., Sofia, Bulgaria.

Burma—Director of Posts, 125 Phayre St., Rangoon, Burma.

Burundi—Agence Philatélique, Boîte Postale 45, Usumbura, Burundi.

Cambodia—*see* French Overseas Agency.

Canada—Philatelic Service, Post Office Department, Ottawa 8, Ontario, Canada.

Canal Zone—Philatelic Agency, Balboa Heights, Canal Zone.

Cape Verde—Postmaster, G. P. O., Praia, Cape Verde Island.

Cayman Islands—Chief Postmaster, Georgetown, Grand Cayman, Cayman Islands, B.W.I.

Central African Republic—*see* French Overseas Agency.

Ceylon—Philatelic Bureau, G. P. O., Colombo, Ceylon.

Chad—*see* French Overseas Agency.

Chile—Director General of Posts and Telegraphs, Department of Posts, International Philatelic Service, Santiago, Chile.

China—Philatelic Department, Director General of Posts, 2 Section I, Changsha St., Taipei, Taiwan, Republic of China.

Colombia—Empresa Nacional de Telecommunicaciones, Servicios Postales, Bogotá, Colombia.

Comoro Islands—*see* French Overseas Agency.

Congo (ex-Belgian)—Philatelic Agency of the Republic of the Congo, 14 Blvd. Maurice Lemonnier, Brussels 1, Belgium.

Congo (ex-French, Middle Congo)—*see* French Overseas Agency.

Cook Islands—Philatelic Bureau, P. O. Box 200, Rarotonga, Cook Islands (South Pacific).

Costa Rica—Director General of Posts, Philatelic Bureau, San José, Costa Rica.

Cyprus—Postmaster General, G. P. O., Nicosia, Cyprus.

Czechoslovakia—Artia, Philatelic Department, P. O. Box 790, Prague, Czechoslovakia.

Dahomey—*see* French Overseas Agency.
Denmark—Postens Filateli, Radhuspladsen 59, Copenhagen V, Denmark.
Dominica—Postmaster, G. P. O., Roseau, Dominica, B.W.I.
Dominican Republic—Agencia Filatélica Dominicana, Apartado 21, Santo Domingo, Dominican Republic.

Ecuador—Director General of Posts, Philatelic Section, Quito, Ecuador.
Ethiopia—Philatelic .Division, Ministry of Posts, Addis Ababa, Ethiopia.

Falkland Islands—Colonial Postmaster, G. P. O., Port Stanley, Falkland Islands (via Uruguay).
Fiji—Postmaster General, G. P. O., Suva, Fiji.
Finland—General Director of Posts, Philatelic Division, Mannerheimintie 11, Helsinki 10, Finland.
France—Receveur Principal des P. T. T., 52 Rue du Louvre, Paris, France.
French Overseas Agency—Agence Comptable des Timbres-poste d'Outre-mer, 85 Avenue de La Bourdonnais, 75-Paris 7e, France.
French Polynesia—*see* French Overseas Agency.
French Southern and Antarctic Territories—*see* French Overseas Agency.
Fujeira—G. P. O., Fujeira, Arabian Gulf (via Bahrain).

Gabon—*see* French Overseas Agency.
Gambia—Postmaster, G. P. O., Bathurst, Gambia.
Germany (West)—Bundesminister für das Post und Fernmelde-wesen, Koblenzer Strasse 81, Bonn 53, Germany.
Germany (Berlin)—Versandstelle für Sammlermarken, Goethe-strasse 2/3, Berlin, Charlottenburg 2, Germany.
Germany (East)—German Democratic Republic.
Ghana—Chief Accountant, Department of Posts, Philatelic Division, Accra, Ghana.
Gibraltar—Colonial Postmaster, G. P. O., Gibraltar.
Gilbert and Ellice Islands—Philatelic Bureau, Central Post Office, Tarawa, Gilbert Islands.
Great Britain—Philatelic Bureau, G. P. O. 2–4 Waterloo Place, Edinburgh, U. K.

Greece—General Direction of Posts, Philatelic Division, 4 Voulis St., Athens, Greece.

Greenland—Order from Denmark.

Grenada—Colonial Postmaster, G. P. O., St. George's, Grenada, B.W.I.

Guatemala—General Director of Posts, Philatelic Division, Guatemala City, Guatemala.

Guinea—Agence Philatélique, Boîte Postale 814, Conakry, Guinea.

Guyana—Postmaster, G. P. O., Georgetown, Guyana.

Haiti—Agence Philatélique Haitienne, Boîte Postale 723, Port-au-Prince, Haiti.

Honduras—Director General of Posts, G. P. O., Tegucigalpa, Honduras.

Hong Kong—Postmaster General, G. P. O., Hong Kong.

Hungary—Philatelia Hungarica, P. O. Box 20, Budapest 5, Hungary.

Iceland—Frimerkjasalan, Director General of Posts and Telegraphs, Reykjavik, Iceland.

India—Presidency Postmaster, Philatelic Bureau, G. P. O., Bombay, India.

Indonesia—Director General of Posts and Telecommunications, G. P. O., Bandung, Indonesia.

Iran—*see* Persia.

Iraq—Postmaster, G. P. O., Baghdad, Iraq.

Ireland—Philatelic Agency, Dublin Postal District, Dublin, Ireland.

Israel—Ministry of Posts, Philatelic Services, Jerusalem, Israel.

Italy—Direzione Generale P. T. T., Servizio 111, Division, IV, Sezione 1, Rome, Italy.

Ivory Coast—Agence Philatélique, Direction des P. T. T., Abidjan, Ivory Coast.

Jamaica—Postmaster General, G. P. O., Kingston, Jamaica.

Japan—Philatelic Agency, Ministry of Posts and Telecommunications, Tokyo, Japan.

Jordan—Philatelic Section, P. T. T., Box 71, Amman, Jordan.

Jugoslavia—Jugo Filatelija, Palmoticeva 2, Belgrade, Jugoslavia.

Kenya—Postmaster General, Box 30301, Nairobi, Kenya.

Korea—Philatelic Agency, P. O. Box 495, Central Post Office, Seoul, Republic of Korea.

Kuwait—Philatelic Section, G. P. O., Fahed Salim St., Kuwait, Arabian Gulf (via Bahrain).

Laos—*see* French Overseas Agency.

Lebanon—Receveur Principal des Postes, Beirut, Lebanon.

Lesotho (ex-Basutoland)—Postmaster, Maseru, Lesotho (via South Africa).

Libia—Director General of Posts, Tripoli, Libia.

Liechtenstein—Official Stamp Retail Service, 9490 Vaduz, Liechtenstein.

Luxembourg—Direction des Postes, Office des Timbres, Luxembourg.

Macao—Postmaster, Macao (via Hong Kong).

Madagascar—Agence Philatélique, Direction des Postes, Tananarive, Malagasy Republic.

Malawi—Postmaster General, G. P. O., Blantyre, Malawi.

Malaysia—Postmaster General, Kuala Lumpur, Malaysia.

Mali—Philatelic Service, Bamako, Mali.

Malta—Postmaster General, G. P. O., Valetta, Malta.

Mauritania—Bureau Philatélique, Boîte Postale 99, Nouakchott, Mauritania.

Mauritius—Postmaster General, G. P. O., Port Louis, Mauritius.

Mexico—Dept. de Emisiones Postales, Dirección Gral. de Correos S. C. T., Tacuba #1, Palacio Postal, Mexico 1, D. F., Mexico.

Monaco—Office of Postal Administration, Department of Finance, Monaco.

Montserrat—Chief Postmaster, Plymouth, Montserrat, B.W.I.

Morocco—Post Office Department, Financial Services, Rabat, Morocco.

Mozambique—Postmaster, Lourenço Marques, Mozambique.

Muscat—Postmaster, Muscat Post Office, Muscat (Arabian Gulf).

Nauru—*see address under* Australia.

Nepal—Philatelic Bureau, G. P. O., Káthmandu, Nepal.

Netherlands—Netherlands Postal Service, Philatelic Section, Kortenaerkade 12, The Hague, Netherlands.

Netherlands Antilles—Philatelic Service, G. P. O., Willemstad, Curaçao, Netherlands Antilles.

New Caledonia—*see* French Overseas Agency.

New Hebrides (English & French)—Condominium Postmaster, Port Vila, New Hebrides.

New Zealand—Director General, G. P. O., Wellington C1, New Zealand.

Nicaragua—Philatelic Agency, P. O. Box 325, Managua, Nicaragua.

Niger—Office des P. T. T., Niamey, Niger Republic.

Norfolk Island—*see address under* Australia.

Norway—Postverkets Frimerkesalg til Samlere, Oslo, Norway.

Pakistan—Karachi G. P. O., Philatelic Bureau, Karachi, Pakistan.

Panama—General Administration of Posts, Philatelic Section, Panama City, Panama.

Papua and New Guinea—Philatelic Section, G. P. O., Port Moresby, Papua-New Guinea.

Paraguay—General Directorate of Posts, Philatelic Section, Asunción, Paraguay.

Persia—Central Administration of Posts, Philatelic Section, Sepah Ave., Tehran, Iran.

Peru—Chief of Philatelic Postal Museum, G. P. O., Lima, Peru.

Philippines—Bureau of Posts, Philatelic Division, Manila, Philippines.

Pitcairn Islands—Postmaster, Pitcairn Islands.

Poland—Ruch, P. O. Box 154, Warsaw 1, Poland.

Portugal—Philatelic Bureau, Rua de São José 20, Lisbon, Portugal.

Portuguese Colonies—Agencia General do Ultramar, Rua de São Pedro de Alcantara 81, Lisbon, Portugal.

Portuguese Guinea—Postmaster, Bissau, Portuguese Guinea.

Qatar—Department of Posts, Philatelic Bureau, P. O. Box 820, Doha, Qatar (Arabian Gulf).

Ras al Khaima—Postmaster General of Ras al Khaima, P. O. Box 99, Ras al Khaima, Trucial States (via Bahrain).

Réunion—*see* French Overseas Agency.

Rhodesia—Philatelic Bureau, Private Bag 199H, Salisbury, Rhodesia.

Romania—Cartimex, Philatelic Department, Box 134–135, Bucharest, Romania.

Russia—Mezhdunarodnaja Kniga, G-200, Moscow, U.S.S.R.

Rwanda—Philatelic Agency of Rwanda, 14 Boulevard Maurice Lemmonier, Brussels 1, Belgium.

Ryukyu Islands—Ryukyu Philatelic Agency, G. R. I., Naha, Okinawa, Ryukyu Islands.

Sabah—Director of Posts and Telegraphs, Jesselton, Sabah (ex-North Borneo).

St. Helena—Chief Postmaster, G. P. O., Jamestown, St. Helena.

St. Kitts-Nevis—Chief Postmaster, Basseterre, St. Christopher, B.W.I.

St. Lucia—Chief Postmaster, G. P. O., Castries, St. Lucia, B.W.I.

St. Pierre & Miquelon—*see* French Overseas Agency.

St. Thomas & Prince Islands—Postmaster, St. Thomas (São Tomé), St. Thomas & Prince Islands.

St. Vincent—Postmaster, Kingstown, St. Vincent, B.W.I.

Salvador—Director of Posts, Avenida España 2, San Salvador, El Salvador.

Samoa—Chief Postmaster, G. P. O., Apia, Western Samoa.

San Marino—Ufficio Filatelico Governativo, San Marino (via Italy).

Sarawak—Director of Posts and Telegraphs, G. P. O., Kuching, Sarawak.

Saudi Arabia—Division of Posts and Telegraphs, Philatelic Section, Mecca, Saudi Arabia.

Senegal—Philatelic Agency, Director of Posts, Dakar, Senegal Republic.

Seychelles—Postmaster, Central Post Office, Victoria, Mahe, Seychelles.

Sharjah—Postmaster General, G. P. O., Sharjah, Persian Gulf (via Bahrain).

Siam—Posts and Telegraph Department, G. P. O., Philatelic Division, New Road, Bangkok, Thailand.

Sierra Leone—Postmaster General, G. P. O., Freetown, Sierra Leone.

Singapore—Postmaster General, Singapore.

Somalia—Minister of Economic Affairs, Philatelic Service, Mogadiscio, Somalia.

Somali Coast—Receiver of Posts, Philatelic Service, Djibouti, Somali Coast.

South Africa—Philatelic Section, G. P. O., Pretoria, South Africa.

South-West Africa—Director of Posts and Telegraphs, P. O. Box 287, Windhoek, South-West Africa.

Spain—Director General of Posts and Telecommunications. Philatelic Service, Plaza de las Cibeles, Madrid, Spain.

Sudan—Director of Posts, Philatelic Section, Khartoum, Sudan.

Surinam—Postal Administration, Philatelic Bureau, Paramaribo, Surinam.

Swaziland—Department of Posts and Telegraphs, Mbabane, Swaziland (via South Africa).

Sweden—Post Office Philatelic Agency, Fack P. F. F. S., Stockholm 1, Sweden.

Switzerland—Philatelic Service Office, P. T. T., Parkterrasse 10, Bern, Switzerland.

Syria—Receiver General of Posts, Damascus, Syria.

Tanzania—Postmaster General, P. O. Box 9070, G. P. O., Dar es Salaam, Tanganyika.

Thailand—*see* Siam.

Timor—Postmaster, Dili, Timor.

Tonga—Chief Postmaster, G. P. O., Nukualofa, Tonga.

Trinidad & Tobago—Postmaster General, G. P. O., Port of Spain, Trinidad, B.W.I.

Tunisia—Receveur Principal des Postes, Tunis, Tunisia.

Turkey—Direction Generale des P. T. T., Ankara, Turkey.

Turks & Caicos Islands—Chief Postmaster, G. P. O., Grand Turk, Turks Islands, B.W.I.

Uganda—Director of Posts, Philatelic Division, P. O. Box 231, Kampala, Uganda.

Umm al Qiwain—Post Office, Umm al Qiwain, Arabian Gulf (via Bahrain).

United Arab Republic—Postal Authority, Philatelic Office, Cairo, U. A. R.

United Nations—United Nations Postal Administration, United Nations, New York 10017.

United States—Philatelic Sales Unit, City Post Office, Washington, D. C. 20036.

Upper Volta—Agence Philatélique, Direction des Postes, Ouagadougou, Republic of Upper Volta.

Uruguay—Dirección General de Correos, Division Servicio Internacional, Montevideo, Uruguay.

Vatican—Secretary, Philatelic Department, Vatican City, Italy.

Venezuela—Director General of Posts and Telegraphs, Philatelic Section, Caracas, Venezuela.

Viet Nam—*see* French Overseas Agency.

Virgin Islands—Chief Postmaster, Road Town, Tortola, British Virgin Islands.

Zanzibar—Chief Postmaster, G. P. O., Zanzibar, Tanzania.

Eight stamps of eight newly christened countries whose designs have about them the exoticism of and fascination with the far-off suggested by their very names

CHAPTER 14

Country Names Change

SINCE WORLD WAR II, many colonies which have achieved independence have adopted new names. Some colonies and countries have changed names without altering their status. The outstanding name switches follow:

Current Name—Old Name
Botswana—Bechuanaland Protectorate
Burundi—Part of Ruanda-Urundi (Belgian East Africa)
Congo (ex-French)—Middle Congo
French Polynesia—French Oceania
Ghana—Gold Coast
Guinea—French Guinea
Guyana—British Guiana
Lesotho—Basutoland
Malagasy Republic—Madagascar
Malawi—Nyasaland Protectorate
Malaysia—Fed. of Malaya, North Borneo and Sarawak
Mali—French Sudan
Morocco—French and Spanish Morocco
Netherlands Antilles—Curaçao
Portuguese Guinea—Guinea
Rhodesia—Southern Rhodesia
Rwanda—Part of Ruanda-Urundi (Belgian East Africa)
Sabah (part of Malaysia)—North Borneo
Somalia—Italian Somaliland
Tanzania—Tanganyika and Zanzibar
United Arab Republic—Egypt; Syria (1958–61)
West New Guinea (West Irian)—Dutch New Guinea
Zambia—Northern Rhodesia

Index

Acknowledgment of receipt stamp, 7
Adhesive, 7
Afghanistan: philatelic literature, 117
Airmail, airpost, 7
Airmails: philatelic societies, 30–31
Alaska: Alaskan Collectors Club, 31
Albania: Albanian Philatelic Society, 31; philatelic literature, 117
Albino, 7
Algeria: philatelic literature, 117
American Bar Association Journal, 159
American Philatelic Congress Book (1956), 116
American Society of Magazine Photographers, 154
American Stampless Cover Catalog, 172
Aniline color, 7; *see also* Fugitive color
Antigua: philatelic literature, 117
Arc roulette, 26
Argentina: philatelic literature, 117
Armantides, John, 157
Armantides, Patricia, 157
Armenia: philatelic literature, 117
Arrows, 8
Ascension: philatelic literature, 117
Australia: *Australian Stamp Monthly,* 55; philatelic literature, 117–118; philatelic societies, 31; *Philately from Australia* (magazine), 57; *Stamp News* (magazine), 60; *see also* South Australia
Austria: *Austria-Philatelist* (magazine), 55; philatelic literature, 118; philatelic societies, 31
Authorized delivery stamps, 8
Autographs: Universal Autograph Collectors' Club, 31

Backstamp, 8
Bahamas: philatelic literature, 118
Bahamas 1959 commemoratives, 166–167
Barbados: philatelic literature, 118
Barred stamp, 8
Barrick, Reuben K., 144
Basutoland: philatelic literature, 118
Bâtonné paper, 8
Battle of New Orleans stamp, 153
Belgian Congo: Belgian Congo Study Circle, 32; philatelic literature, 119
Belgium: *Balasse Magazine,* 56; Belgium Study Circle, 32; philatelic literature, 119
Bermuda: philatelic literature, 119
Bicolored stamps, 8
Bilingual stamps, 8
Bisect, 8
Blocks, 8
Bogus stamp, 8
Bolivia: philatelic literature, 119
Booklet pane, 9
Booklets: philatelic societies, 32
Booklist on philately, 116–143
Bosnia: philatelic literature, 119
Boston University Philatelic Library, 116

Brady, Mathew, 146
Brazil: Clube Filatelico do Brasil, 32; philatelic literature, 119
British Commonwealth: philatelic literature, 120; philatelic societies, 32; *see also* individual countries
British North America: British North America Philatelic Society, 32; *see also* Canada
British Solomon Islands: philatelic literature, 120
Brizendine, Mrs. Virginia, 145
Brooks, Charles A., 150
Bureau of Engraving and Printing, 150, 152, 155, 157
Bureau prints, 9
Burelage, 9
Burma: philatelic literature, 120
Burnell, William R., 150, 159

Cachet, 9
Canada: *Canadian Philatelist* (magazine), 56; philatelic literature, 120–121; philatelic societies, 32
Canal Zone: philatelic literature, 121
Canceled to Order (C.T.O.), 9
Cancellation, 9; duplex, 12; grid, 15; killer, 16; manuscript, 18; mute, 19; numeral, 20; packet, 21
Cancellations: fraudulent removing of, 167; philatelic societies, 33; special, 171
Cape of Good Hope: philatelic literature, 121

Cardboard, 9
Carriers' stamps, 9
Catalogue, how to use, 92–98; *see also* Scott Catalogue
Cayman Islands: philatelic literature, 121
Centering, 9
Center lines, 9
Ceylon: Ceylon Philatelic Society, 33; philatelic literature, 121
Chalky paper, 9–10
Charity stamps, 10; *see also* Semipostal stamps
Charity stamps and seals: Christmas Seal and Charity Stamp Society, 33
Chile: philatelic literature, 121; Sociedad Filatélico de Chile, 33
China: China Philatelic Society of London, 33; philatelic literature, 122
China, Red: absence of stamp listings for, 165–166
Churchill, Winston, 151
Cinderella Stamp Club, 44, 170
Citizens' Stamp Advisory Committee, 144–145, 147, 148
Clark, Richard Lyon, 151–152
Classic (stamp issue), 10
Classification of exhibitions, 67–68
Clean-cut perforation, 10
Cleaned stamp, 10
Cleary, Joe, 147
Cleveland School of Art, 146
Cliché, 10
Coated paper, 9–10
Coils, 10
Collection, value of, 174
Collections, preparing for exhibition, 61–68
Collectors Club of New York, 116
Collectors Club of Seattle, 116
Colombia: Club Filatélico de Barranquilla, 34; philatelic literature, 122

Color: aniline, 7; changing or fading, 170–171; fugitive, 14; misplaced, 166
Color changeling, 10
Color names, lack of uniformity, 172–173
Color trials, 10
Comb perforation, 10
Commemorative issue, definition of, 10
Compound perforations, 10–11
Confederate States (U.S.): philatelic literature, 142
Control mark, 11
Cooper Union, New York, 158
Costa Rica: philatelic literature, 122; philatelic societies, 34
Cottrell press, 147, 159
Counterfeit, 11; *see also* Bogus
Countries, recent name changes of, 185–186
Cover, 11; first day, 14; first flight, 14; on, 20; patriotic, 21
Covers: philatelic societies, 34; stampless, 27, 172
Creamer, Joseph S., Jr., 147, 152
Crease, 11
Cuba: absence of stamp listings under Castro, 165–166; philatelic literature, 122
Currency exchange, 48–54
Cut cancellation, 11
Cut to shape, 11
Cut square, 11
Cyprus: philatelic literature, 122
Czechoslovakia: Czechoslovak Philatelic Society of North America, 34; philatelic literature, 122

Davison, Mr. and Mrs. George W., 150
Deak & Co., 48
Definitive issue, 11
Demonetized stamp, 12
Denmark: *Frimaerkesamleren* (magazine), 56; philatelic literature, 123

Design, stamp: definition, 12; distinguished from margin, 12; essay, 13; Prominent Americans series of 1966, 144–159
Designers, index of, 160–163
Diamond roulette, 17
Die, 12
Die, reproducing by electrotype, 12
Digest of International Law (Moore), 158
Dintaman, Arthur W., 155, 157, 159
Dohanos, Stevan, 144–145
Dominican Republic: philatelic literature, 123
Double impression, 12
Double paper, 12
Dry printing, 12
Duplex cancellation, 12
Duty plate, 12

Early impression, 12
Ecuador: philatelic literature, 123
Egypt: philatelic literature, 123; philatelic societies, 34
Einstein stamp of 1966, 153–155
Eire, *see* Ireland
Electrotype, 12
Embossed stamps, 13
Encased postage stamps, 13
England, *see* Great Britain
Engraved stamps, 13
Engraver's proof, 13
Enoch Pratt Free Library, Baltimore, 116
Entire, 13
Error, 13
Essay, 13
Essays and proofs: Essay-Proof Society, Inc., 34
Estonia: philatelic literature, 123
Exhibition pane, *see* Souvenir sheet
Exhibition of stamps, 61–68
Exhibits, classification of, 67–68
Expertize (to), 13
Express delivery stamps,

13; *see also* Special delivery stamps

Fabris, Josef, 156
Face value, 13
Facsimile, 13
Fakes, 13–14; *see also* Bogus; Counterfeit
Falkland Islands: philatelic literature, 123–124
Famous Photographers School, 154
Fantasy, 14, 170
Faries, Belmont, 145
Fiji: philatelic literature, 124
Fine perforation, 14
Finland: philatelic literature, 124
First day cover, 14
First day covers, agencies for purchasing, 175–184
First flight cover, 14
First issues of the world (1840–1966), 69–71
Fiscal (stamp), 14
Flat plate, 14
Foreign currency exchange, 48–54
Forgery, *see* Counterfeit; Fake
Frame, 14
France: France and Colonies Philatelic Society, 35; *L'Echangiste Universel* (magazine), 56; *L'Echo de la Timbrologie* (magazine), 56; *Le Monde des Philatélistes* (magazine), 57; philatelic literature, 124–125
Franchise stamps, 14
Frank, 14
Freak, 14
Free Library of Philadelphia, 116
French colonies and offices abroad: France and Colonies Philatelic Society, 35; philatelic literature, 125; *see also under* individual countries
French Morocco: philatelic literature, 125
Fugitive color, 14; *see also* Aniline color

Gabon: philatelic literature, 125
Gambia: philatelic literature, 125
General philatelic societies, 45
Germany: *Die Sammler-Lupe* (magazine), 57; philatelic literature, 125–126; philatelic societies, 35
Glossary of philatelic terms, 7–29
Goldbeater's skin, 14
Granite paper, 14
Great Britain: *Gibbons Stamp Monthly,* 56; philatelic literature, 126–127; *Philatelic Magazine,* 57; philatelic societies, 35; *The Philatelist* (magazine), 57; *Philately* (magazine), 57; *Stamp Collecting* (magazine), 57; *Stamp Magazine,* 60; *see also* British Commonwealth; British North America
Greece: Hellenic Philatelic Society of America, 35; philatelic literature, 127
Grenada: philatelic literature, 127
Grid cancellation, 15
Grill, 15
Grilled gum, 15
Gripper cracks, 15
Guatemala: philatelic literature, 127; philatelic societies, 35
Guggenheim Museum, New York, 156, 157
Guide dots, 15
Guide lines, see Center lines
Gum, 15
Gum, original, 20
Gum breaker bars, 15
Gutters, 15

Haiti: philatelic literature, 127–128
Hall, Haines, 146, 147
Halsman, Philippe, 154–155
Handstamped, 15
Harrow perforation, 15

Hatching, 15
Head plate, *see* Duty plate
Hejaz: philatelic literature, 128
Heligoland: philatelic literature, 128
Hinge, 16
Honduras: philatelic literature, 128
Hong Kong: Hong Kong Study Circle, 35; philatelic literature, 128
Humphrey, Hubert H., 150
Hungary: imperforates, 169–170; philatelic literature, 128
Houdon, Jean Antoine, 150
Hyde, Wilbur Rundles (Bill), 146–147, 148–150
Hyphen hole, 16

Iceland: philatelic literature, 128
Identification of stamps, 99–115
Illustrators Club of San Francisco, 146
Imperforate, 16
Imperforates, foreign, 169–170
Imperial Hotel, Tokyo, 156
Impression, 16
Imprint, 16
India: *India's Stamp Journal,* 56; *Philatelic Journal of India,* 57; philatelic literature, 128–129; philatelic societies, 35–36
India paper, 16
Inscription, 16
Institute for Advanced Studies, Princeton, 153
Insurance stamps, 16
INTERPEX, 62
Interrupted perforation, *see* Syncopated perforation
Invert, 16
Iraq: Iraq Philatelic Society, 36
Ireland: Eire Philatelic Association, 36; philatelic literature, 129
Israel and Palestine: Einstein stamp, 155; phila-

telic literature, 129; philatelic societies, 36
Italy, Italian states and colonies: *Il Collezionista* (magazine), 56; philatelic literature, 129–130; Vatican Philatelic Society, 44

Jamaica (B.W.I.): Jamaica Study Group, 36; philatelic literature, 130
Japan: *Kitte Shumi* (magazine), 56; philatelic literature, 130; philatelic societies, 36
Johnson & Son Administration Building, 156
Joint line pair, 16
Jones, Robert L., 150, 152, 155, 157
Jugoslavia: philatelic literature, 131

Kaiser-Wilhelm Physical Institute, Berlin, 153
Kent, Roger, 145
Killer, 16
King, Admiral Ernest, 151
Knife, 16
Korea: Korea Stamp Society, 37; philatelic literature, 131
Korea, North: absence of stamp listings for, 165–166

Laid paper, 17
Late fee stamp, 17
Latvia: philatelic literature, 131
Laufer, Tom, 158
Leeward Islands: philatelic literature, 131
Letter sheet, 17
Liberia: philatelic literature, 131
Libraries containing philatelic literature, 116
Library of Congress, 116
Lidman, David, 145
Liechtenstein: Liechtenstein Study Circle, 37; philatelic literature, 131
Lincoln stamp of 1966, 146–147

Line pair, 17
Ling Po, 156, 157
List of Philatelic Handbooks (publication), 116
Lithography, 17
Lithuania: Lithuanian Philatelic Society, 37
Locals, 17
Lozenge roulette, 17
Luminescent stamps, 18
Luxembourg: Luxembourg Philatelic Study Club, 37; philatelic literature, 131–132

McCloskey, Victor S., Jr., 157
Madagascar: philatelic literature, 132
Magazines of philately, 55–57; *see also under* individual countries
Malaya: Malaya Study Group, 37; philatelic literature, 132
Manchukuo: philatelic literature, 132
Manhattan project, 153
Manila paper, 18
Manuscript cancellation, 18
Margin, 18
Marginal inscriptions, 18
Marginal watermarks, 18
Masons: Masonic Stamp Club of New York, Inc., 37
Master plate, 18
Match and medicine stamps, 18
Matejka, Dr. James J., Jr., 145
Meters and slogans: philatelic societies, 37
Meter stamp, 18
Mexico: philatelic literature, 132; philatelic societies, 37
Mildner, Howard C., 150, 152, 155, 157
Military stamps, 18
Miller, Robert L., 150, 152, 155
Miniature sheet, 18
Mint, 19
Mirror print, 19

Misplaced colors, 166
Misstrike, 19
Mixtures, 19
Moiré, 19
Monaco: philatelic literature, 132
Montenegro: philatelic literature, 132
Moore stamp of 1966, 158–159
Mount, 19
Multiple watermark, 19
Mute cancellation, 19

Name changes of countries, colonies, 185–186
Natal: philatelic literature, 133
National Gallery of Art, Washington, D.C., 150
Native paper, 19
Nepal: philatelic literature, 133
Netherlands and colonies: Netherlands and Colonies Philatelists (club), 38; philatelic literature, 133
New countries, 185–186
Newfoundland: philatelic literature, 133
New Guinea: philatelic literature, 133; *see also* Papua and New Guinea
New Hebrides: philatelic literature, 133
New issues, agencies for purchasing, 175–184
New South Wales: philatelic literature, 133
Newspaper stamps, 19
Newspaper tax stamps, 19
New Zealand: New Zealand Society of Great Britain, 38; philatelic literature, 133
Nicaragua: Sociedad Filatélica de Nicaragua, 38
Norway: *Norsk Filatelistisk Tiddsskrift* (magazine), 57; philatelic literature, 134
Numeral cancellation, 20

Oblique roulette, 20

Obliteration, *see* Cancellation

Obsolete stamps, 20

Occupation stamps, 20

Official seals, 20

Official stamps, 20

Offset (impression), 20

Offset printing, 20

On cover, 20

Ontario College of Art, 153

Orange Free State: Orange Free State Study Circle, 38; philatelic literature, 134

Original gum, 20

Overprint, 20; *see also* Surcharge

Oxidation, 20

Pacific Islands: Pacific Islands Study Circle of Great Britain, 38

Packet, 21

Packet cancellation, 21

Pair, 21

Pakistan: philatelic societies, 38

Palestine, *see* Israel and Palestine

Panama: philatelic literature, 134

Pan-America: Pan-American Collectors Club, 38

Pane, 21

Paper: bâtonné, 9; chalky, 9–10; double, 12; goldbeater's skin, 14; granite, 14; India, 16; laid, 17; Manila, 18; native, 19; pelure, 21; quadrille, 24; ribbed, 25; ruled, 25; safety, 25; silk, 26; silk thread, 27

Papua and New Guinea: Papuan Philatelic Society, 38; philatelic literature, 134; *see also* New Guinea

Paraguay: philatelic literature, 134

Parcel post stamps, 21

Part perforate, 21; value of, 173–174

Paste-up, 21

Patriotic covers, 21

Payne, George A., 147, 155

Peale, Charles Willson, 150

Peale, Rembrandt, 149–150

Pelure, 21

Penalty envelopes, 21

Penny Black, first postage stamp, 69

Percé, see Roulette

Percé en Arc, 26

Percé en lignes obliques, 20

Percé en Losanges, 17

Percé en Points, 22

Percé en Pointes, 29

Percé en scie, 25

Percé en serpentin, 26

Perfins, 21; philatelic societies for, 38–39

Perforate: first perforate stamp, 69; part, 21, 173–174

Perforated initials, *see* Perfins

Perforated margins, 21

Perforates and straight edges, 169

Perforation: clean-cut, 10; comb, 10; fine, 14; harrow, 15; hyphen hole, 16; rough, 25; syncopated, 28

Perforation gauge, 21

Perforations: compound, 10–11; how measured in Scott Catalogue, 166–167

Persia: Persian Study Circle; philatelic literature, 134

Peru: Asociación Filatélica Peruana, 39; philatelic literature, 135

Philatelic agencies, 175–184; ordering through, 175–176

Philatelic agency, definition of, 21–22

Philatelic exhibitions: Philatelic Literature Association, 39

Philatelic literature: books, 116–143; libraries containing, 116; magazines, 55–57; Scott Catalogue, 93–98; *see also under* individual countries

Philatelic Research Society of Oakland, 116

Philatelic Societies, 30–47; advantages of joining, 30; general societies, 45–46; regional societies, 46–47; topicals, 42–43; *see also under* specific subjects and individual countries

Philatelic Society, 150

Philatelic terms, 7–29

Philatelist, definition of, 22

Philately, definition of, 22

Philippines: Asociación Filatélica de Filipinas, 39; *Philippines Journal of Philately,* 57; philatelic literature, 135

Phosphor tagged, *see* Luminescent stamps

Photogravure, 22

Pin perforation, 22

Plate, 22

Plate numbers, 22

Plate proof, 22

Plate variety, 22

Plating, 22

Pneumatic post, 22

Poland: philatelic literature, 135; Polonus Philatelic Society, 39

"Porthole Portrait" by R. Peale, 149–150

Portugal and Portuguese colonies: International Society for Portuguese Philately, 39; philatelic literature, 135

Position blocks, 22

Postage currency, *see* Encased postage stamps

Postage due stamps, 23

Postal administrations, 175–184

Postal fiscal, 23

Postal history: philatelic societies, 39–40

Postally used, 23

Postal stationery: United Postal Stationery Society, 40

Postcards: Metropolitan Postcard Collectors Club, 40

Postmark, 23

Postmarks: philatelic societies, 33
Postmaster General as arbiter of design, 144, 145
Postmasters' provisionals, 23
Precancels, 23; philatelic societies, 40
Prince of Wales (battleship), 151
Princeton University, 153, 154
Printed on both sides, 23
Printers' waste, 23
Printing: dry, 12; lithography, 17; offset, 20; photogravure, 22; rotary press, 25; wet, 29
Private die proprietary stamps, 23; *see also* Match and medicine stamps
Prominent Americans Stamps of 1966, 144–159; Einstein stamp, 153–155; Lincoln stamp, 146–147; Moore stamp, 158–159; Roosevelt stamp, 151–152; Washington stamp, 148–150; Wright stamp, 156–157
Proof, 23
Proofs: Essay-Proof Society, Inc., 35
Provisionals, postmasters', 23
Puerto Rico: philatelic literature, 135

Quadrille paper, 24
Queensland: philatelic literature, 135

Railroad postmark, 24
Recutting, 24
Reconstruction, *see* Plating
Redag, Larry, 146, 147
Redrawn design, 24
Re-engraving, 24
Re-entry, 24
Registration stamps, 24
Regummed stamp, 24
Reissue, 24
Remainders, 24
Repairing, 24
Reperforating, 25

Reply coupons: Reply Coupon Collectors' Society, 40
Reprints, 25
Retouch, 25
Réunion: philatelic literature, 136
Revalued stamp, *see* Surcharge
Revenues, 25; American Revenue Association, 40; how to identify, 170
Rhodesia: philatelic literature, 136; Rhodesian Study Circle, 40
Ribbed paper, 25
Ripple gum, *see* Grilled gum
Romania: philatelic literature, 136
Roosevelt stamp of 1966, 151–152
Rotary press printing, 25
Rough perforation, 25
Roulette, 25; diamond, 17; lozenge, 17; oblique, 20; *percé en losanges,* 17; pin perforation, 22; sawtooth, 25; serpentine, 26; serrated, 26; zigzag, 29
Ruled paper, 25
Russia: philatelic literature, 136; philatelic societies, 40–41; *see also* Ukraine
Ryukyu Islands: philatelic literature, 136; philatelic societies, 41

Safety paper, 25
Saint-Mémin, Charles Fevret de, 148
Salvador: philatelic literature, 136
Samoa: philatelic literature, 137
Sample, 25; *see also* Specimen
Sarawak: philatelic literature, 137; Sarawak Specialists Society, 41
Sawtooth roulette, 25
Scandinavia: philatelic societies, 41; *see also* individual countries
Scott Catalogue: facsimile page, 94; how to use, 93–98; missing numbers in, 168; sampling of stamp queries to, 165–173; supplements, 171–172
Scott's Guidebook to Stamp Collecting (William), 98
Scott's Monthly Stamp Journal, 57, 171–172
Seals, how to identify, 170
Sebastiano, Frank, 153–154
Secret marks, 25
Semipostal stamps, 25; *see also* Charity stamps
Serbia: philatelic literature, 137
Serpentine roulette, 26
Serrated perforation, 26
Serrated roulette, 26
Set, 26
Se-tenant, 26
Seychelles: philatelic literature, 137
Sharpless, Howard, 152
Sheet, 26
Sheets: Miniature Reconstructed Sheet Society, 41
Sheet watermark, 26
Siam: philatelic literature, 137
Sierra Leone, 6 pence of 1859, 69
Silk paper, 26
Silk thread paper, 27
Silurian paper, *see* Granite paper
SIPEX commemorative stamp, 158
Skinned stamp, 27
Society of Typographic Arts, Chicago, 146
Solomon Islands, *see* British Solomon Islands
South Africa: philatelic literature, 137; philatelic societies, 41
South Australia: philatelic literature, 137
Southwest Africa: philatelic literature, 137
Souvenir sheet, 27
Spain and colonies: *Madrid Filatélico* (magazine), 56; philatelic literature, 137–138; philatelic societies, 41

Spanish Civil War Study Group, 41
Special delivery stamp, 27
Specialist, 27
Specialized study groups, 30–47; see also under individual subjects and countries
Special printing, 27
Specimen, 27
Speculative issue, 27
Split grill, 27
Stamp collections, preparing for exhibition, 61–68; classification, 67–68; completeness, 65–66; condition of stamps and covers, 65; monetary value, 65; presentation, 63–64; research, 64–65; topicals, 64
STAMPEX, 62
Stampless covers, 27
Stamps: agencies for purchasing new issues, 175–184; bibliography, 116–143; changing or fading color, 170–171; definitions of terms, 7–29; determining condition of, 11; "Famous Germans" series (1961), 155; first issues, 69–91; identifying, 99–115; inconsistent color names, 172–173; index of designers, 160–163; magazines for collectors, 55–60; misplaced colors, 166; of new countries, 185–186; organizations for collectors, 30–47; preparing for exhibition, 61–68; Prominent American series, 144–159; Scott Catalogue, 93–98; special cancellations, 171; specialized study groups, 30–47; unlisted, 165; see also Philatelic
Stark, Admiral Harold R., 151
Stevens, Roger L., 145
Straight edges, 28, 169
Straits Settlements: philatelic literature, 138

Strip, 28
Sudan: philatelic literature, 138
Surcharge, 28
Surtax, 28
Swaback, Mrs. Vernon, 156
Swaback, Vernon, 156, 157
Sweden: philatelic literature, 138; Svenska Filatelistisk Tidskrift (magazine), 60
Switzerland: Berner Briefmarken-Zeitung (magazine), 56; philatelic literature, 138–139; philatelic societies, 42; Schweizer Briefmarken-Zeitung (magazine), 57
Syncopated perforation, 28

Taliesin West, 157
Tasmania: philatelic literature, 139
Teeth, 28
Telegraph stamps, 28
Tête-bêche, 28
Thailand: Thailand Philatelic Society; see also Siam
Tibet: philatelic literature, 139
Tied stamp, 28
Todhunter, Norman, 145
Tongs, 28
Too late stamp, see Late fee stamp
Topical collections, how to exhibit, 64
Topicals: philatelic societies, 42–43
Transvaal: philatelic literature, 139; Transvaal Study Circle, 43
Trinidad: Trinidad Philatelic Society, 43
Trumbull, John, 150
Tunisia: philatelic literature, 139
Turkey: philatelic literature, 139
Typographed stamp, 29

Ukraine: philatelic literature, 139
United Nations: philatelic literature, 139; philatelic

societies, 43–44
United States: Linn's Weekly Stamp News, 56; Mekeel's Weekly Stamp News, 56; philatelic literature, 140–142; philatelic societies (for U.S. stamps), 44; Stamps (magazine), 60; see also Confederate States
U.S. stamp designers, index of, 160–164
Unlisted stamps (locals, fantasies, bogus, etc.): philatelic societies, 44
Unused stamp, 29
Unwatermarked, 29
Uruguay: philatelic literature, 142; philatelic societies, 44
Used stamp, 29
USSR, see Russia

Variety (stamp), 29
Varnish bars, 29
Vatican: Vatican Philatelic Society, 44
Venezuela: Club Filatélico de Caracas, 45; philatelic literature, 142
Victoria: philatelic literature, 143
Viet Nam, North: absence of stamp listings for, 165–166
Vignette, 29
Virgin Islands: philatelic literature, 143

Walker, John, 145
War tax stamps, 29
Washington stamp of 1966, 148–150
Watermark, 29
Wet printing, 29
Wheatley, David, 156
Wiener, Kurt, 145
Wiram, Kenneth C., 157
Wove bâtonné, see Bâtonné paper
Wright, Olgivanna, 157
Wright stamp of 1966, 156–157

Yugoslavia, see Jugoslavia

Zigzag roulette, 29

The Sikh Separatist Insurgency
in India